Forty Books for Forty Years

An informal history of Boydell & Brewer

Forty Books for Forty Years

An informal history of
Boydell & Brewer Group Ltd 1969–2009

Richard Barber

The Boydell Press

First published 2009
The Boydell Press, Woodbridge

ISBN 9781843835547

The Boydell Press is an imprint of Boydell & Brewer Ltd
PO Box 9, Woodbridge, Suffolk IP12 3DF, UK
and of Boydell & Brewer Inc
668 Mount Hope Ave, Rochester, NY 14604, USA
website: www.boydellandbrewer.com

A CIP catalogue record for this book is available from the British Library
This publication is printed on acid-free paper

Typeset by Richard Barber
Cover and illustration layout: Helen Barber
Copy-edited by Fionnuala Jervis, who has as always kept the author
on the strait and narrow

Printed in Great Britain by CPI Antony Rowe,
Chippenham and Eastbourne

Contents

OTHER IMPRINTS

FORTY IMAGES

Preface

When authors come to us and express concern as to what reviewers will say about their book, our advice is often to set out the controversial topic in the preface, so as to disarm their criticism by pointing out the problem. Skilfully done, this saves them from weakening their argument by ifs and buts, and from looking over their shoulder as they write. So I must declare at the outset that this is an informal history, written largely from memory (though I have checked the dates, barring a few places where there are sadly lapses in our records). If I have remembered wrongly, I offer my apologies; I know that much has been left out, and that is deliberate, as I have no desire to be tediously comprehensive. But I hope that what follows will be of interest as a record of a corner of the publishing and academic world in late twentieth-century England. It may also raise a smile on the way; that is part of the intention.

INTRODUCTION

'If I'd realised that 95% of publishing is about accounts, I would never have started this firm.' That was how John MacCallum Scott summed up his experiences at Pall Mall Press, where he had given me my first job. This is a book about the other 5% – or perhaps more than that – of publishing. It is a history of Boydell & Brewer Ltd told through a tiny selection of the titles it has published in the last forty years, and I make no apologies for presenting it from my own viewpoint. Small, and sometimes not so small, publishing firms are very much driven by people; the public aspect is the authors and editors, but the nature of the business also requires very special skills from the supporting departments.

If you were to build an ideal business model, a publishing firm would not be the starting point: a huge number of totally diverse products whose source is individuals who very often have quite different agendas from that of the business, and complex production problems. What follows presents really only one aspect of the operation: our interface with the authors and public. There is another story to be written, but one which would be much nearer to an orthodox business history. After forty years, Boydell & Brewer remains stubbornly individualistic, with our own warehousing and computer systems .

Some of the formal history of Boydell & Brewer does need to be told, briefly, to set the scene. The company was formed as Leviathan Press Ltd in 1969, only to discover that the name had already been registered by C. Northcote Parkinson, an early business guru whose book *Parkinson's Law* is still sometimes quoted.[1] This meant that we had the problem of finding another name. Since all of us were working full-time, mostly for other publishers, we did not want to use our own. The discussion was long and

---

[1] One of Boydell & Brewer's principles has been that proper, on-page, footnotes are 'A Good Thing', so this is how we shall proceed. Parkinson's Law stated that the board of a company would take a few minutes to approve a million pound development plan, and then argue for an hour about the cost of building a cycle shed.

heated, and we paused for a while to get our breath. On the wall there was an eighteenth-century engraving inscribed 'Published by John Boydell'. This seemed as good a name as any, and so we became The Boydell Press.[2] What we did not know until later was that Boydell had a highly successful career; he was master of the Stationers' Company,[3] and later Lord Mayor of London, but he then embarked on a highly ambitious scheme for an illustrated Shakespeare, for which he commissioned new paintings from the leading artists of the day, which would be engraved for his edition. He built a gallery in Pall Mall in which the originals were to be displayed, but this grandiose project was derailed by the onset of the Napoleonic wars, and he had to apply to parliament to dispose of his paintings by lottery, since the engravings had failed to sell.

The Boydell Press started with a modest £100 in capital, and has so far neither achieved John Boydell's dramatic success, nor succumbed to his dramatic fall. The intention of the original directors was to publish sponsored books, an area in which two of them had considerable expertise, and in which they are still active today.[4] Unfortunately, by the time we were up and running, the oil crisis of 1972–3 had struck, and big companies no longer had money to spare for schemes on the lines of *The National Westminster Book of Opera*. So we were unlikely to bring off such lucrative projects, and our first clients were more modest: indeed some of the early books have to be labelled as vanity publishing.[5]

The direction the firm took was really determined by personal considerations. Shortly after we started, one director went bankrupt over a theatre venture,[6] and departed. He was replaced by Helen Tolson, who was working for André Deutsch at the time; we married in 1970 and moved to Suffolk in 1972.

With the move, the firm found its first niche, one of the succession which we have occupied over the forty years. Niches are excellent things, but you have to move to the next niche at the right moment. A fortunate chance led us into

---

[2]   Even this was not unique; it was also used by Iain Bain, who published limited editions of engravings; but we managed to coexist without problems.
[3]   His magnificent portrait by Sir Joshua Reynolds hangs on the stairs at Stationers' Hall.
[4]   Jeremy Greenwood of JJG Publishing, and Julian Platt of Third Millennium.
[5]   See *Lesudden House* below.
[6]   But not before the firm had daringly put up £25 to back a play by Robin Maugham – and lost it all. It may not sound much now, but it was a quarter of our capital.

FORTY BOOKS FOR FORTY YEARS

local publishing, when we acquired *Suffolk Churches*[7] and a few other titles from Norman Adlard Ltd, an Ipswich printer-publisher. The relative success of these led us to look for more of the same, and for a time our staple was the three local series, *Suffolk Library*, *Norfolk Library*, and *Essex Library*. But other developments were also afoot. We had been able to move to Suffolk because I could see a year or two's secure income from my writing. I had been an author before I took up my first publishing job, and my first two books were out of print, having appeared ten years earlier.[8] I was in touch with an American publisher, John Mladinich, who worked for Barnes & Noble and later Rowman & Littlefield, and he agreed to buy a quantity of each; and so our more serious publishing began. The connection gave us a sound entry into the US market, and we learnt a great deal from both him and his successor, Homer Dickens.

These tentative beginnings of a history list were quickly overshadowed by a development which was to bring us firmly into the academic field, though the country and sporting list was to be our mainstay for another decade.

I first met Derek Brewer in 1970 when, as a very green young editor at George Bell & Sons, I enlisted him to edit a volume on Chaucer in a series on 'Writers and their Background'. Among some distinguished books, Derek's was probably the best of the set. By the time it appeared, The Boydell Press had been formed, and I told him of our project. We had only just managed to publish our first two or three books when he asked me to lunch in the Cambridge Arts Theatre, during which he outlined his dissatisfaction with academic publishing and his desire to start an imprint of his own. With all the confidence of a newly established publisher, I suggested that we should set up a company in his name, and would undertake all the administrative work and distribution on his behalf. D. S. Brewer Ltd came into existence in 1972, and the two firms existed side by side until 1976, when it became clear that the energy put into accounting and managing two separate entities would be better employed elsewhere, and that it was logical to merge them to form Boydell & Brewer Ltd.

It takes a long time to build a list on the kind of resources we had at our disposal, and looking back, it is clear that 1978–79 was the moment when

---

[7] Bold indicates that a title is described below.

[8] When I told my agent, the formidable Juliet O'Hea of Curtis Brown, that I was thinking of becoming a publisher, she said firmly 'Don't make your hobby your job'. But I took no notice. The two books were *Arthur of Albion* (see *Arthurian Legends* below) and *Henry Plantagenet*.

the business really became a serious entity. In that year, we started three series which are still central to the operation, *Arthurian Studies*, *Chaucer Studies*, and *Anglo-Norman Studies*. *The Green Man* was the first of many unlikely titles,[9] which if not best-sellers, performed solidly in spite of (or perhaps because of) their improbable subjects: *Fashion in the Age of the Black Prince*[10] was another such contribution in 1980. And the first of thirteen volumes of the *Catalogue of the Pepys Library at Magdalene College, Cambridge* appeared in 1978.

At the end of our first decade, we were still in business, not entirely certain which way we were going, but happy to seize any opportunity. We had just moved from hand-written invoices direct to a computer. Even in those days programming was a headache: a week or two after we had started to use the system, we needed to do a credit note. Nothing doing … So we rang the software firm, who said that we hadn't asked for credit notes and there was no room for the minus sign. Not long after, there was a fire above the room where the computer was kept, and although the fire brigade carefully covered the machine with a tarpaulin, it got slightly wet. With huge trepidation, I opened the cover, and dried it out with blotting paper. After this, I became *de facto* the company's computer maintenance man and programmer.[11] I should have been warned off when a programmer came in to help me, arrived at seven one evening, and was still there in the morning, saying he didn't like to break off in case he forgot the way he was going to solve the problem. Programmers today don't run on midnight oil and black coffee in the way they used to, but it can easily become an obsession.[12]

By 1985, we were beginning to have a solid academic list, but this did not deter us from other ventures. We started a series of paperback reprints, not the most original thing to do at the time, which really consisted of favourite

---

[9] Simon Jenkins, writing in *The Times*, called it 'The rarest, most recondite and fascinating art book, which is a folklore and magic book as well …'.

[10] See *The Green Man* below

[11] Computers could be a very long footnote, or perhaps a series of footnotes, as a kind of running commentary on the firm's progress. Suffice to say that until 2009 all our programs were written in house, and were sometimes the objects of envy on the part of much grander publishers, who said 'But our system can't do that!' Later, we also tweaked a British Telecom system called X-25, used by multi-nationals like Ford for stock control, and hitched it up to PCs in the UK and the US. The engineer who came to service it was more than a little surprised to find it being used to link two very small offices indeed.

[12] I remember the individual who confidently sold a program called *The Last One* – because it was the last program you would ever need, since it could write any program you wanted: a single magic floppy disc. But of course it didn't work.

out of print books suggested by the directors and their friends. There were some very obscure items alongside excellent forgotten authors such as Arthur Morrison, and the occasional surprise such as *Augustus Carp Esq*. This gave us a foothold in the bookshops which was useful when we did come across big trade books. We were lucky in 1979 with *The Arthurian Legends*, which remains our biggest-selling book, and we also did well with *The Normans* in 1984. Hugh Tempest-Radford,[13] who had wide experience of the printing business, had joined us by this time, and found excellent printers for us. Lack of expertise in costing meant that, given the huge discounts required by the book clubs, the margins were pitiful. Perhaps it was fortunate, for we might have been tempted into a more general arena where we could not really compete. But steady sales of small quantities of our history titles to book clubs became a staple of our list.

The other area which enabled us to grow and to consolidate was Japan. Derek Brewer's contributions to the list were often surprising,[14] but he provided a link which enabled us to move confidently into a larger-scale academic publishing operation. He had taught in Japan from 1956 to 1958, at a time when English studies were blossoming there, and many of his friends and students were later to become senior figures in Japan's academic world. One of his students, Toshiyuki Takamiya was to play an important role in the development of the D. S. Brewer list. He was in Cambridge as a research student from 1975 to 1978, and was responsible for the first volume in the **Arthurian Studies** series, as well as the first manuscript facsimile we published. Thirty years later, the compliment was returned with the publication of a well-merited volume of essays in his honour.[15]

When Helen and I went to Japan in 1987 Derek's name was a kind of password not only to the academic world but also to the great bookselling firms of Maruzen, Kinokuniya, Yushodo and Kitazawa. We found ourselves, as very small players in the publishing world, dining with the chairman of Maruzen, proud of his firm's recent acquisition of a copy of the Gutenberg bible. It established connections which were invaluable to us over the next twenty years, until the decline of the Japanese economy reduced their once insatiable appetite for books on medieval English literature. At times as much as a quarter of our overall business was with Japan.

13 Now publishing elegant art books under the Unicorn Press imprint.
14 See *Graptolites*.
15 See *The Mediaeval Book and the Modern Collector*.

The US had been a modest market for us in the early years, and many of our books were taken on a consignment basis for distribution rather than sold to a US publisher; initially Rowman & Littlefield looked after the distribution side, as well as buying the occasional title, but in 1984 we were approached by Longwood, who had the excellent idea of offering not just distribution but a staff member responsible for the management and publicity for the list. I went for the first time to the US, and found myself in the depths of New Hampshire; the offices were in Wolfeboro, a delightful Victorian resort town with a splendidly unrestored early-nineteenth-century inn, and the warehouse was in a former textile mill in Sanford, Maine. The idea behind the Longwood system was excellent, but it was not matched by their handling of the business. Within three years, they were unable to pay us, and it was only the initiative of Martin Spencer at Edinburgh University Press, who also used them, that saved us. He and David Croom of Croom Helm invited us to join them as Longwood's three largest creditors, and we worked out a solution which ensured that we got our money out in returning for continuing to work with them. John Varey, who founded the Tamesis imprint, was also a Longwood customer; he knew Derek, and when he heard of the scheme, asked if we could take on his US sales and thus join in the arrangement. This was the unexpected benefit of what threatened to be a disaster, leading eventually to the acquisition of Tamesis.

However, even after the outstanding money had been repaid, it was clear that Longwood's business model was not sound. By this time, I had learned something about US business practice. Some of it was surprising, such as discovering that the bank where we were opening an account had just fifty or so branches, because state law in New Hampshire did not then allow banks based outside the state to trade there. The decision was taken to set up an American subsidiary, and I went to Portsmouth, Maine, to see a law firm which had been recommended to me. As I drove in, I stopped and asked a passer-by for directions, and said I was looking for Tybursky & Watson in Cate Street. 'Oh,' was the reply, 'you're the Englishman coming to see Tom Watson. I'm Tybursky.' So Boydell & Brewer Inc was formed; but the firm was no more than a trading entity for several years.

It was obvious that we needed a presence in the US. Looking at the efforts of other firms to establish themselves there, simply setting up shop as ourselves was self-evidently not going to be enough. During one of those conference conversations which just occasionally result in a wonderful book or an exciting project, I wondered whether it might be possible to offer to run a press for an American university, without financial subsidies, and on terms which would provide a base for Boydell & Brewer's US operations. What I did not know at the time was that Brian Thompson, the provost of the University of Rochester, was looking for a firm who might, in his words, 'be willing to become a strategic business partner'. Two medievalists from Rochester, Tom Hahn and Russell Peck, knew Derek, and suggested that a meeting should be arranged. We duly travelled to Rochester, and Brian took us to dinner. He began by introducing the 'token American'; of the five people round the table, four were English. Derek and Brian discovered a common enthusiasm for the English grammar schools of the 1940s where they had been educated, and the relationship quickly developed into a partnership which has stood us – and the University – in good stead ever since.

Once the contract was in place,[16] we needed a US manager. It was a tall order: we could not afford a large salary, and we had to have someone familiar with the UK publishing world. The best person for this formative stage was more likely to be English than American, but that raised the huge question of visas. Fortunately, one of our authors, James Carley, who had already helped us to establish contact with Rochester, had rented a house in Cambridge from a visa specialist in the US embassy; there was a little-known but very useful exchange visa, which allowed UK firms to send people to subsidiaries if they had specialist knowledge of the workings of the company. We found Robert Easton, who had already spent some time selling expensive facsimiles in the US from an English base, and after six months with us in the UK, we filled in the complex E1 documentation, and he was issued with the necessary papers.

We now had a twin base, with an office in the University and distribution in Wolfeboro; Robert set about establishing the Press as a presence in the academic community, under Brian's direction, and dealing with the problems at Longwood. A year or two later, Longwood collapsed, but we had already found another distributor. However, the stock had to be extracted from the former mill in Sanford, and taken to Fitchburg in Massachusetts: fortunately there was not a great deal of it, and Robert loaded a U-haul van, having got into the more or less abandoned warehouse, and drove it to PSSC, who still handle our business. Longwood had done our sales and accounting, so we now had to set up invoicing as well as the rest of the financial services.

[16]   See p.83-4 below for the details of the arrangement, which still appears to be unique among university presses.

By then our account manager at Longwood, Kai Norris, had joined Robert in Rochester, so the sales side was taken care of; the downside was that they married soon afterwards, and the two of them came to England. With the appointment of Robert's replacement, the staff of the US subsidiary – there were now five employees – became wholly American. Its history, like those of the other imprints which joined the group, is told at the end of the book.

The headcount in England was also growing. We had operated up to now out of the former farm office attached to the house, but were able to buy the neighbouring farmyard buildings; this was partly because one night there was a huge crash, all the pheasants woke up and swore loudly as they flew off, and the next morning we saw that the old stackyard had collapsed. We took the building nearest to the house, and converted this in 1985. Vanda Andrews, who joined us shortly after the office was completed, told us a few days after she arrived that her grandfather had once worked there – when it was a cowshed. Within a year or two, we had to build again, and the resulting rather warren-like offices saw us through for nearly twenty years, increasingly cramped but very pleasant in their way: roses over the front door and a passing hoopoe for the twitchers to be seen out of the east window looking towards the sea. In 2003 we moved to Melton, near Woodbridge, to a handsome building which had once been part of a mental hospital, and stands in parkland overlooking a golf course, with a weeping prunus planted by Princess Alexandra in front of it, and a four hundred year old oak tree to one side.

We were by now publishing a very respectable number of books for a small company, a little below 60 in 1987 under the Boydell & Brewer imprints, with a handful of books produced for learned societies. To generate this quantity of projects we relied heavily on freelance editors and later on academic advisers and series editors. Kevin Crossley-Holland, who had been a colleague at Macmillan[17] and had wide contacts in the literary world, joined us when he came to Suffolk to write as a freelance author, and we explored many ambitious – and over-ambitious – projects for books which drew on our medieval strengths but were aimed at the general market. His *Beowulf* [18] was an example of this genre, and he and I went to Frankfurt for the Book Fair for a number of years. Frankfurt was still a place where contracts were signed

[17]   Helen and I had both worked at Macmillan in the 1960s; she was working in publicity when I joined the production department there after leaving Pall Mall Press. Kevin had been editorial director of Gollancz and was now a freelance writer like myself.
[18]   See *The Age of Sutton Hoo* below.

on the spot, and the talk was of the latest international bestseller rather than of which company was being sold to whom and the intricacies of electronic publishing, and it was possible for us to market foreign rights to good effect. We had – indeed still have – a splendid Italian agent, Ezio Rovida, who seemed to be able to sell obscure medieval titles to Italian publishers, and over the years sold one book to two different publishers in succession: it appeared under two different titles, which must have confused the bibliographers.[19] It was a heady time, when everything seemed possible, and the jackpot of an international co-edition and a main choice for a book club was within reach.[20]

But reality soon crept in again, and we found the trade market growing harder and harder to break into, as booksellers became chains and wholesalers demanded higher margins. There was a conscious decision to turn away from the trade market, but to make what we could from it; so the emphasis shifted towards the academic books which might have a trade sale. These cross-over books needed new selling techniques, and we were actually led into one of our most profitable selling methods by an author. Pamela Tudor Craig wrote a wonderful book on the thinking behind Renaissance masterpieces, *The Secret Life of Paintings*,[21] and at the launch party insisted that not only were the books sold, but that we gave her guests a discount. I managed to turn up late, having misread the address on the invitation, to find Gwyn Headley, whom we had hired to do the publicity, smiling broadly and patting his pockets – and not a book in sight! He had sold the lot in the first twenty minutes, and thereafter, despite the Net Book Agreement, we sold at a discount at book launches and then at conferences. Fortunately we were small fry, and could get away with it. Now, with the Net Book Agreement gone, we have no such problems: but everyone else does it too.

On the academic side, we were fortunate in attracting enthusiastic supporters such as Toshiyuki Takamiya. Our high profile in such areas as Arthurian Studies made us many friends, and Derek's own pre-eminence in Chaucerian scholarship was another source of goodwill. This was territory where mainstream publishers were reluctant to tread, and we had a clear run for a decade, before the university presses, perhaps because of our success, came back into the fields which they had abandoned. Our one disadvantage was not being a university press imprint, because publication was an essential

19   *The Knight and Chivalry* became both *Il Mondo della Cavalleria* and *Cavalieri del Medioevo*.
20   See Jonathan Raban's account of our Frankfurt activities under *Tournaments*.
21   With Richard Foster; it was based on a television series.

route to academic advancement, and for a long time there was a prejudice against independent publishers, whose standards of selection and editing were seen as inferior. We did not always succeed in keeping up our standards, but our record compared very favourably with that of the larger presses, and we insisted on keeping footnotes where they belonged – at the foot of the page – when the big firms were relegating them to the end on grounds of economy.

As we moved increasingly into the academic world, conferences came to loom large in our operations, notably the famous gathering of medievalists at Kalamazoo each year, which now attracts over 3000 delegates, and its equivalent at Leeds, the International Medieval Congress. There are plenty of tales to be told about conferences, but one stands out in the memory particularly, the International Arthurian Congress at Rennes in 1984. It had been taken on by a member of faculty rather against the University's wishes, and seemed to have some kind of poltergeist attached as a result. I arrived on a very small plane from Gatwick, which staggered across the Channel and immediately made an unscheduled touch-down before continuing to Rennes. The co-pilot handed round the local newspapers, which was fortunate. When we reached the conference accommodation (having worked out that it was at Rennes IX – a surprisingly wide choice of universities in one town, it seemed) there were high locked steel gates, behind which a welcoming banner could be seen. Fortunately the local paper had featured the Congress, and mentioned that there would be a concert in a church that evening; so we found the church and the other delegates. It continued in this vein, the highlight being an excursion in the legendary forest of Brocéliande. Rennes was sweltering in record temperatures, and we looked forward to a stroll through forest glades. Instead, we got out at a point where all the trees had been felled but not cleared, and had to pick our way across them: four strong men carried a delegate in a wheelchair through the chaos. And the rest of the forest was as bare as Macbeth's blasted heath, and much hotter. After a couple of hours, we came to a French village dozing in the Sunday afternoon, and about sixty Arthurians, dying of thirst, burst into the local bar, to the astonishment of the half-dozen locals present. Somewhat strengthened, we continued to the spring which features in the Arthurian romance of *Yvain*: its magic feature was that if a knight poured water from the spring onto the stone, a thunderstorm ensued, and the story was that when the first Arthurian congress visited the spring in 1948, someone daringly poured the water, and a thunderstorm duly broke out, to general satisfaction. This time we had no such luck: bathing our feet in it was a poor substitute. And so it went on: an attempt to show Eric Rohmer's *Perceval le Gallois* had to be abandoned because the film broke so often, but humour also broke in – at a hotly contested contentious election, the scrutineer read out the votes, and looked up with a smile at the end as he announced 'and one for Merlin'. We badly needed a little of his magic by the end of the event.

I was once asked to write the history of an institution (my old college at Cambridge) which was intended to run to the present day. I was happy enough to explore the events of the past, but writing about the present is a very different skill, particularly in a small and highly personal organisation; and the history was never completed. I have the same hesitation about Boydell's recent history, which is very much work in progress.

The most conspicuous change has been the shift in emphasis from a trade list with an academic interest, to an academic list which is still capable of handling good trade books when they come up as a by-product of our academic operations. And there is no doubt that the firm is no longer amateur, but highly professional. Both these trends began in the 1980s, but it is only since the first acquisition of another imprint, that of Tamesis in 1995, that they have really shaped what we do.

In a sense, the history of Boydell since 1989 is a history of acquisitions and start-ups, all directed at the academic world. The history of the four imprints added in the last twenty years is told in brief at the end of this book; Camden House came on board in 1998, and James Currey in 2008. As well as these, we developed York Medieval Press with the University of York within our medieval list, which is now a successful imprint running to nearly forty titles since 1997. And last but not least there was the agreement with the Victoria County History in 2001, an enterprise which took us back where we started, to local history, but at a vastly more cerebral level.[22]

With each of these firms and imprints we acquired considerable new expertise; and we were also fortunate in our outside editors, particularly Peter Sowden on modern and maritime history, Stephen Taylor on religious history and Bruce Phillips on the music side.[23] As our involvement in medieval history grew, we acquired excellent series editors who also brought in good titles. There is not enough space to list all the good friends of the press who have

22   See p.68 below
23   See p.63 below

helped to build our list; most of them are also authors, so perhaps the benefit has been mutual. And we have steadily added to the list of learned societies for whom we publish: at the present count there are fourteen in our catalogues.

The current team is almost equally divided between people who have spent all their publishing lives with us and recruits from outside with a much more diverse range of experience. Hopefully this is a recipe for success, and we can continue our track record of making a modest profit each year (with only one exception to date). Years ago, Investors in Industry, now the venture capital giant 3i, made their smallest ever investment by buying a stake in the firm; we bought them out when they decided that bigger fish fried better, but I think that we have proved that we were as sound as they thought we were, if not as spectacularly successful as they had hoped.

To conclude, what is it that gives Boydell & Brewer Group Ltd its particular character? Derek was not the only publisher to be dissatisfied with the university presses; John Varey, whom we helped over the Longwood debacle, had preceded him in founding Tamesis. We took on the UK distribution for Tamesis, and had a seat on the Tamesis board, so when he found the business too burdensome to run – his range of interests was extraordinary – we agreed an amicable takeover. Jim Hardin in South Carolina had started Camden House for similar reasons. Again, we took on his distribution, first in the UK and then in the US. He suggested we might like to buy him out, while he continued to handle the editorial side. And the University of Rochester Press also started from dissatisfaction with the status quo, in this case with the traditional structure of American university presses and their often considerable cost to the academy. James Currey has a mission which is both academic and social, to produce good books on Africa, and to make them as widely available in Africa itself. So from one imprint founded by an academic, we now have five high profile academic lists within Boydell & Brewer, as well as the academic element in the Boydell Press imprint. This is reinforced by the learned societies whom we distribute, the most notable being the Early English Text Society with a list going back to the 1860s, all of which we have made available again, and the Victoria County History, dating from queen Victoria's Jubilee, whose backlist we rescued and continue to reprint steadily. The fact that much of it is available free online does not seem to have stifled demand for the handsome red VCH volumes. All this gives us strong and deep roots in the academic community.

As to the future, we try – and I think largely succeed – to maintain the high standards of academic publishing across our entire list, while retaining the flexibility to innovate and explore new structures of publishing. We shall need all our skills and experience in the coming years, but we start our fifth decade in good shape: independent, with dedicated and excellent staff, and owned by shareholders who have indicated their commitment to the company's ideals by setting up an ownership trust for the employees.

The uncertainties facing publishing in the coming years are all too familiar: the immediate problems of recession and its aftermath, the threats and opportunities of new media, the trend towards instantly accessible but far from reliable information on the web. What we have to remember is that the medium is *not* the message: the message, the considered and measured voice of the academic community, is what we exist to purvey and facilitate. In the future our role will gradually – not suddenly – begin to focus not only on the physical book but also, in a wider sense, on the function that publishing has always filled in the world of learning, of being the link between author and audience. We can not only link author and audience, but we can be a gateway, a filter, which ensures the quality of the content, and also which enables scholars to present their content in the best and most appropriate way. To do this, we need to be inventive: for instance, we should perhaps offer a publishing liaison service which goes far beyond the problem of how to present a thesis in book form, but actually helps authors to improve the quality of their content and deals with such issues as the presentation of draft material in electronic form for circulation and discussion. The future may be threatening, but even the elephant in the room – by which I mean Google – is perhaps less dangerous than we think. Google's plans are hugely ambitious, but I can only judge by results: in my own field, in the seven years since they have started, they have digitised almost nothing of the huge amount of valuable out of copyright material. From my viewpoint, I wonder if the elephant is really there? While we wait to see if the electronic revolution actually materialises, we can use recent technology to do things which were not previously possible, for example to produce a lot of useful out of copyright material in print on demand form. There may be similar short-term opportunities as things move on. If we can stay flexible and alert, I hope Boydell & Brewer will prosper for some time to come, continuing that mixture of commerce and altruism which is a proud tradition of the publishing world.

FORTY BOOKS

FOR FORTY YEARS

*The forty books which follow are drawn from the Boydell Press and
D.S. Brewer lists, and from some of the learned societies
and institutions which they represent; the other imprints
in the group have their own histories at the end.*

THE AGE OF SUTTON HOO

Edited by Martin Carver

Anglo-Saxon history, 1992

The Sutton Hoo excavations had already become part of local legend by the time we came to Suffolk, and the place itself was mysterious, accessible only by a rough footpath. Once Martin Carver's excavations began, however, it was back in the public eye, and when the International Society of Anglo-Saxonists visited Sutton Hoo on 21 August 1985, we entertained them there. It was a fine afternoon, and photos show distinguished scholars reclining on the mounds enjoying a glass of sparkling Saumur and pistachio ice-cream. Our Anglo-Saxon list had only just been launched, and it was an auspicious start.

Two years later, we returned to Sutton Hoo for a reading from Kevin Crossley-Holland's *Beowulf*, which was appearing in a new illustrated version. It was a wet October, and the skies only cleared at the last minute, to give us a spectacular red sunset with dark clouds as Kevin read first in Anglo-Saxon and then in modern English. The audience was small because of the uncertain weather, and stood around braziers which grew brighter as darkness fell. Those who ventured out for the occasion still remember it as an extraordinarily dramatic and evocative evening.[24]

As Martin Carver's work at the site drew to a close, and after we had agreed to publish *The Age of Sutton Hoo*, I went to see him there, and after walking round the site, he came to a green tarpaulin on the ground. Pulling it back, he revealed the first horse-burial to be found in England, a young prince buried with his favourite steed, with provisions for both horse and man on their journey to the next world. The skeletons lay, movingly, just as they had been uncovered a few days earlier, before their removal for closer examination.

ISBN 9780851153612, paperback, 424 pp, £25/$50[25]

[24] Another memorable setting for a party was Orford Castle, which we rented for £25 to celebrate Norman Scarfe's *Suffolk in the Middle Ages*. One of the requirements was that we insured the building against all perils; I approached our insurers with this strange request with some trepidation, but they took the view that if it had stood for 800 years, nothing much was likely to happen to it on one particular day, and the fee was no more than the cost of issuing the policy.

[25] Page sizes are 234 x 156 mm unless otherwise stated.

ANGLO-NORMAN STUDIES

Founding editor: R. Allen Brown

Early medieval history, 1979–

This was the first series of conference proceedings which the Boydell Press published. It began life with the cumbersome title *Proceedings of the Battle Conference on Anglo-Norman Studies*. The conference was the brainchild of Allen Brown, whom I had met during committee meetings of the Suffolk Records Society. The first conference was held in 1978, and he was insistent that the proceedings should appear in time for the following year's conference,[26] and that has been consistently achieved over the ensuing thirty years under five different editors. The conference has travelled abroad, to Caen, Palermo, Dublin, Glasgow and Gregynog; although Battle is its spiritual home, the change of title was appropriate, for it is now the recognised international forum for Anglo-Norman historians.

The success of *Anglo-Norman Studies* led to three further series which give similar coverage for the whole of the history of England between the Norman Conquest and the advent of the Tudors. *Thirteenth Century England* began at Durham in 1985, followed by *The Fifteenth Century* and *Fourteenth Century England* in 2000. *Fourteenth Century England* is in a sense the odd one out, as it does not have a conference of its own, but instead draws on papers given at the two great medieval conferences at Leeds and Kalamazoo. Nigel Saul portrayed the fourteenth century as something of a Cinderella in medieval studies when he reviewed the first volume to appear, a situation which the series has helped to remedy. Just as in Victorian times trade followed the flag, so many of the authors of articles in these series have gone on to write books for us.

Latest volumes:
Anglo-Norman Studies 31, 9781843834731, hardback, 224 pp, £45/$90
Thirteenth Century England 12, 9781843834472, hardback, 224 pp,
£70/$135
Fourteenth Century England V, 9781843833871, hardback, 208 pp, £50/$95
The Fifteenth Century VIII, 9781843834144, hardback, 216 pp, £50/$95

---

[26]   He also refused to have an index, on the grounds that scholars should read the book if they wanted to find out what was in it; but he had the advantage over the rest of us of a superb, almost photographic, memory.

THE ANGLO-SAXON CHRONICLE

General editors: David Dumville and Simon Keynes

Anglo-Saxon history, 1996–

One of the first D. S. Brewer books was Eric Stanley's *The Search for Anglo-Saxon Paganism*, which led us into the problems of typesetting Anglo-Saxon. Orthodox letterpress setting was far too expensive for our modest budgets, so we used an IBM electronic typewriter with a golf-ball head. The result was just about acceptable, but we had to solve the problem of the special characters required. A printer friend came up with the answer, a specially adapted head where characters which we did not need were filed off, and very small line blocks of the Anglo-Saxon characters were glued on in their places, using a slow-setting glue which allowed for adjustment to the positioning. This method served us well for a number of years, and enabled us to publish titles which would otherwise have been uneconomical because of the requirement for 'special sorts', as the letterpress equivalents were called.

The Anglo-Saxon Chronicle followed in 1983. It was conceived by its general editors, David Dumville and Simon Keynes, as a large project, to print all six manuscripts of the Anglo-Saxon Chronicle itself and many of the works deriving from it, as well as reconstructions of the original texts which had formed the basis of the manuscripts. It was a huge and slow undertaking, and may not yet be at an end; the most recent volume appeared in 2004.

When we published the first volume, we got extensive publicity, including a piece by Philip Howard in *The Times* headed 'King Alfred burns cakes – latest'. His source for this 'hot off the press' message was the manuscript of the Chronicle in the Parker Library at Corpus Christi College, Cambridge; in order to see it, he gallantly fought his way from London through a snowstorm in the best tradition of a reporter on a mission.[27]

Latest title: The Anglo-Saxon Chronicle: 7. MS E, edited by Susan Irvine, ISBN 9780859914949, 360 pp, frontispiece, £70/$135

---

[27]   He was disappointed that he could not touch the precious artefact; rigorous manuscript conservation was still something of a novelty, but the librarian, Ray Page (who subsequently became a Boydell author), insisted that only scholars studying the text could handle it.

ART AND POWER

Roy Strong

Art history, 1984

Sir Roy Strong's study of Renaissance festivals began life as a series of lectures at Hull, and was originally published as *Splendour at Court* by Weidenfeld & Nicolson in 1974, in a format aimed at a general market. The illustrations were integrated with the text, and there were no footnotes; and the book was disastrously embroiled with a printer's strike which meant that the bound copies were locked up in a factory for nine months. Ten years later, we published a revised edition which addressed Roy Strong's dissatisfaction with the original presentation, as well as giving him the opportunity to revise the text in the light of a flood of new scholarship on the subject. Usually the transition is from academic to popular version rather than the other way round, but the idea that an academic presentation does not necessarily put off the reader was very much our philosophy then, and still is now. The book was given footnotes, and the illustrations, instead of being treated as decorative elements, were placed together at the end of the book and considerably increased in number. This gave the book the academic credibility which the earlier edition had lacked, and made the text more accessible.

Most important of all, the book was retitled; and in this new form it was one of our most successful ventures. At the Frankfurt Book Fair, we displayed books where we had sold rights with a handwritten header saying 'Rights sold' and a list of the languages for which agreements had been signed. This technique – I think unique at the time – proved excellent, because publishers looking for books to translate were attracted to titles which had already had such sales in other languages. *Art and Power* eventually appeared in French, German, Italian, Spanish and Japanese, which for an academic book from a small firm was a considerable achievement.

ISBN 9780851152479, paperback, 204 pp, 115 illustrations, £17.99/$34.95

THE ARTHURIAN LEGENDS

An Illustrated Anthology
Edited by Richard Barber

Arthurian literature, 1987

In the more leisurely early days of the firm, I had time to put together an Arthurian anthology. *The Arthurian Legends* was our most successful book in terms of volume sales. It was a striking book, printed in two colours throughout in its original form, though later versions had to be reduced to one colour to achieve the necessary price for paperbacks and book clubs. There was nothing quite like it on the market, at a time when Arthurian enthusiasm was at its height. And it included one medieval text, on the death of Arthur, which had not previously appeared in translation. It was embellished by a number of Pre-Raphaelite illustrations, for which there was a growing vogue.[28]

The Arthurian Legends was sold to both the Ancient History Book Club and the History Book Club in the US, and reprint editions for Barnes & Noble and Crown Books followed; the total sales were somewhere not far short of half a million – I fear that our record keeping on this point was not sufficiently detailed to be certain.

The Arthurian Legends was followed by a revised edition of my early *Arthur of Albion*, which we had reprinted with the US publisher Rowman & Littlefield in 1971. *King Arthur in History and Legend* was launched with a tour of the west country Arthurian sites for journalists and reviewers. A mini-bus set out on a tour designed to travel full circle, from the sites associated with Arthur as myth to the places named in the small and sketchy evidence for the historical Arthur. As luck would have it, we ran into a wet day of the kind that only the south-west can provide. We peered at Cadbury Castle from beneath our umbrellas, and journeyed on to Glastonbury, with the supposed grave of Arthur, and to Malmesbury, where Guinevere retired to a nunnery.

Near Glastonbury, an American member of the party asked Jamie George, owner of the Gothic Image bookshop, about the idea that the signs of

---

[28] I remember reluctantly deciding at the time that I could not possibly afford £2000 for George Frampton's early twentieth century portrait bust of Iseult, to see it go for well into six figures twenty years later.

the zodiac could be traced in landmarks around the town. He politely agreed with her, but added as an aside to me 'And you could see Snow White and the Seven Dwarfs if you wanted to.' Perhaps it is this all-inclusiveness that makes the Arthurian legend so popular – there is room for high academic argument, great creative literature, and zany myth-making under the Arthurian umbrella: and a mere wet day did not spoil the fun.

Out of print

ARTHURIAN STUDIES

General editor: Norris Lacy

Arthurian literature, 1987

Arthurian Studies began in 1979 with *Aspects of Malory*, edited by Toshiyuki Takamiya and Derek Brewer, an auspicious start for a series which thirty years later numbers seventy-eight volumes on all aspects of the Arthurian legend and its literature. The third volume in 1981 was the result of an early foray into humanities computing by Cedric Pickford and Rex Last of Hull University: *The Arthurian Bibliography* ran to eight hundred pages, with a cut off date of 1978. It was input with the help of three members of a training programme for the long term unemployed, paid for by the Manpower Services Commission. The foreword is an interesting piece of computer history, which describes the struggles with the mainframe computer at Hull, and its inability to print in lower-case, which meant that the entire book is in block capitals. But despite this it was a success, and has had two supplements to date, bringing it up to 1998.

The series has included editions of Chrétien de Troyes, a translation of Wolfram von Eschenbach's *Parzival*, John Masefield's Arthurian poems, and notable works on Arthurian art by Muriel Whitaker and Barbara Tepa Lupack. Its main thrust, however, is the Arthurian monograph: the most notable is Peter Field's *The Life and Times of Sir Thomas Malory*, a masterly survey of the historical evidence about the author of the *Morte Darthur*. Malory is a mainstay of the series, with a dozen volumes including *A Companion to Malory*. Derek Brewer edited the equally important *Companion to the Gawain-Poet*. And fittingly, as the bibliography of books and articles on Arthurian matters grows exponentially – a single volume of the bibliography issued by the International Arthurian Society contains as many items as five such volumes in the 1970s – one of the recent volumes is *A History of Arthurian Scholarship*, whose editor, Norris Lacy of Penn State University, is also the current editor of the series.

Latest title: The Grail, the Quest and the World of Arthur edited by Norris J. Lacy, ISBN 9781843841708, 34 pp colour plates, throwout, £50/$95

AUGUSTUS CARP ESQ

Sir Henry Howarth Bashford

Fiction, 1985

In 1982, we launched a series called *Bookmarks*, intended to reprint classics which for one reason or another had fallen out of favour. It was eventually renamed *Bookmasters* because the original series title was already in use by a book marketing company, and counsel's opinion went against us when we were threatened with legal action. The choice of titles was a bit haphazard, and an experienced publisher would have been more systematic and rigorous about the selection. I think the low point was reprinting Charles Morgan's *The Fountain*, then one of my favourite novels, getting a full page review from John Bayley in the *Times Literary Supplement*, and selling three copies in the following fortnight. But there were some unexpected successes, among them *Augustus Carp Esq by Himself* (1985). Frank Muir called it 'one of those little master-pieces which seem to pop up from nowhere', and it was a wonderfully funny comic portrait of a self-appointed guardian of bourgeois morals, 'President of the St Potamus league for moral purity'. In fact it was the work of the honorary physician to George VI, Sir Henry Howarth Bashford, whose other books give little hint that he might have this unexpected comic talent.

It caught on immediately, and by the time of the Frankfurt Book Fair that year we made it a feature of our stand. This we shared with a wonderful Dutch publisher, De Harmonie, run by Jaco Groot, whose fund of good stories (and alcohol) made the annual pilgrimage to Frankfurt a pleasure rather than a penance. He seemed to know everyone, whereas we knew a very few specialists, and he made a habit of selecting one of our books which he would set out to promote to his friends. We had sent him a copy of *Augustus Carp Esq* earlier in the year, and he had taken it to Greece on his annual holiday there. Here the cartoonist Glen Baxter, who was staying with him, seized on it, and read it aloud on the beach to some friends. They noticed that other holidaymakers were gradually shifting their beach towels nearer so that they could listen. (One of them, before joining the group, was heard to ask 'Is this a cult?') By the third day, as the audience grew, he had dug out a child's clock, which he set up to announce the time of the next reading, and a photo of this duly appeared at Frankfurt. Jaco showed the photo to Peter Carson of Penguin

Books, and this so intrigued him that he bought the paperback rights. And it subsequently became one of a series of collaborations with the Folio Society, which included Maria Perry's *Word of a Prince*, my edition of Aubrey's *Brief Lives* and *Bestiary*. But the last word must go to Kenneth Williams, who read it as a serial on Radio 4:

'I had a great deal of trouble at the microphone … most of it was caused by the need to stifle my laughter at the po-faced humour of the writing; mind you, the response to the broadcasts was so enthusiastic that we realised the effort had been well worth while.'

Out of print

THE BURY BIBLE

Introduction by R. M. Thomson

Manuscript facsimile, 2001

The facsimiles we have published have largely been working facsimiles, designed for scholars who are interested in the text; the expense of colour would have made them prohibitive for all but a handful of libraries. Our earliest venture in this field was an attempt, supported by Allen Brown, to undertake a new facsimile of Domesday Book, which we proposed to print in red and black only. However, the enormous cost and the difficulties of filtering out the red lettering with the technology of the day, meant that we had to withdraw, though not before Geoffrey Martin, then Keeper of the Public Record Office, had taken the momentous decision to disbind Domesday Book, which had been elaborately but very tightly rebound less than fifty years before. This paved the way for Editions Alecto's monumental publication.

The Bury Bible offered different challenges. Much of the text was plain, with a handful of illuminated initials: but there were spectacular pages of paintings which were some of the greatest masterpieces of English twelfth-century art. They were largely invisible to all but a few scholars, as the manuscript could only be displayed with two pages open in a secure glass case. We decided to issue a partial facsimile, in full colour, which would make these images available to a wider public at full size, together with the fine illuminated initials. Even using the largest size of paper we could obtain, however, we still had to marginally reduce the original in order to make it fit. The dimensions also posed photographic problems, which were only solved when the HUMI project for reproducing manuscripts digitally, based at Keio University and led by Toshiyuki Takamiya, became involved, and proposed to produce a full version in digital form. A specially built camera was brought from Japan, with a mounting designed to hold the manuscript and to allow very precise focus and exposure. The result was a set of images of the highest quality; the lighting was superbly done, and we were able to reproduce even the gold leaf accurately and without the problems of reflection. (Many facsimiles, in my view, are spoiled by the application of flat gold leaf or the use of gold ink, because a parchment leaf is never flat, but gives the gold light and shade.)

The facsimile was accompanied by an introduction by Rod Thomson on the production of the bible and on the artist responsible, Master Hugh, whose perfectionism ran to insisting that the coloured illumination was done on an extra thickness of specially purchased Scottish parchment, pasted in place so that the colours would not show through on the other side of the leaf.

The East Anglian associations of the Bury Bible meant that we were able to launch the facsimile in the cathedral at Bury St Edmunds, next to the ruins of the great abbey for which it was made.

ISBN 9781843840664, 510 x 350 mm, 102 pp, 48 colour illustrations, 31 black and white illustrations, paper boards, £95/$180

BYGONES

Dick Joice

Local history, 1976

Local publishing inevitably led to an association with the local television station, Anglia TV in Norwich, and we quickly struck up an excellent relationship with them, particularly with Dick Joice, presenter of their highly successful 'Bygones' series of programmes.

'Bygones' had come about because Dick had been parachuted into the job of presenting Anglia programmes by his employer, Lord Townshend, who was the chairman of the new company. In those days, the presenter had no backup if there was a problem in the studio, and one day Dick ran out of all the formal announcements and time-fillers. He remembered that he had been sent something by a member of the public that morning, and pulled out from his drawer a potato which looked like a rabbit, and talked about that until the studio was ready. From then on a steady stream of oddities came to him from his audience across the region, particularly old gadgets and mystery objects. They became the substance of a regular half-hour programme, and also found their way into his personal collection of 'bygones', now at Holkham Hall. The programme was hugely popular, and had been going for some years when we came on the scene. We published four small books based on programmes from the series, whose titles give a snapshot of how the concept had evolved: *Lady Margaret Barry and Mrs Gertrude Smith*, an 'upstairs, downstairs' view of Edwardian life, *Barns and Granaries*, on farm architecture, *Arthur Randell, Fenman*, and Dick himself on his collection, *Talking about Bygones*. These were packaged in a slipcase – with hindsight, not a practical idea! – and very hesitantly we printed 4,000 copies for publication in late October. Bertrams were just coming to the fore as a book wholesaler, and as they were based in Norwich, Elsie Bertram took a couple of hundred to start with. We had sold out in a fortnight, but this presented a real problem. The slipcases were assembled by hand by a family in the village, and the original 4,000 had been a major task: now we needed more, urgently, and even the eleven-year-old twins of the family were enlisted. By Christmas we had sold another 6,000 copies, and I had become accustomed to the run to Norwich with urgently needed stock. I am glad to say that one of the twins – and her family – still does our catalogue mailings thirty years later. *Out of print*

CALENDAR OF INQUISITIONS POST-MORTEM, 6–10 HENRY V, 1418–1422

David Crook

Medieval history, 2002

In 2000, the Public Record Office (now The National Archives) approached the firm to see if we would be prepared to take on the publication of the Calendars of medieval records. The Stationery Office, which had published them since the nineteenth century, had been reorganised and was no longer interested in continuing the series. The business of the medieval government was usually set down on huge parchment manuscripts in the form of rolls. These were made up of a set of individual pieces of parchment sewn in a vertical chain. Each membrane, as these sewn pieces are called, was then stitched through the head, and the whole thing is rolled up. In the old Public Record Office in Chancery Lane, if you wanted to read a roll, a kind of stepladder was wheeled out. To the left was a smooth board, to the right steps with a writing desk. The Latin roll was lifted onto the board area, and parted at the top so that half of it was allowed to fall on either side of the stepladder. It was a laborious exercise, and the Calendars offered a short cut to discovering what the contents were; each entry was summarised or 'calendared', usually in English, and the volume was provided with an index.

The present set of Calendars began in 1891, and it was only after the Second World War that the pace of work began to slacken; new demands on the archives meant that maintaining an expensive team of highly-trained scholars within the office was an increasing problem. When we started to publish Calendars, several were done by the old method, and in one case at least the text was handwritten. But the advent of computer editing meant that it became feasible for the Calendars to be scholarly projects within university history departments, and for the results to be published both electronically and in paper form (as with the *Parliament Records of Medieval England*). The first of these dual publications was the *Calendar of Fine Rolls* for the reign of Henry III. Fines were payments which were in effect for favours granted by the king or for a certificate that a 'final' agreement had been reached in a lawsuit. With the growing interest on the part of genealogists, the demand for access to these records is rising. But it is not always that simple: the older paper volumes have a wide range of spellings of individual names, and it is difficult to be sure that all such spellings have been checked. In some cases there may be twenty variants of a single name. One day, perhaps, a vast unified index may be compiled.

These printed editions are now increasingly important, as original documents from the National Archives are gradually being removed for storage in the salt mines at Nantwich in Cheshire, despite the protests of the academic community, and are no longer readily available to scholars.

ISBN 9780851158990, hardback, 480 pp, £135/$230

CATALOGUE OF THE PEPYS LIBRARY

General editor: Robert Latham

Bibliography, 1978–1984

In 1976, a proposal for the publication of a full catalogue of the famous library assembled by Samuel Pepys and bequeathed by him in 1703 to Magdalene College, Cambridge, was put to the Cambridge University Press. They hesitated about undertaking the project, perhaps in part because there had been an unsuccessful attempt to produce such a catalogue, starting in 1914 and ending incomplete with only four volumes published in 1940. Robert Latham, who by then had already produced the complete text of the new edition of the *Diary*, turned to Derek Brewer to see if D. S. Brewer would publish it. An agreement was signed for the publication of seven volumes, and the first appeared in 1978. When the final volume was published in 1984, the original seven volumes had swelled to sixteen, including a five-volume facsimile of Pepys's unique collection of contemporary ballads. For an enterprise which had been regarded as somewhat risky at the outset, this was an extraordinary expansion. But the material in the library was very diverse, ranging from printed books to prints and drawings, maps and calligraphy, as well as important naval manuscripts, and of course the manuscript of the diary itself. In addition, the bindings required description, and the original catalogue, a pioneering effort on Pepys's part and still useful today, was reprinted in facsimile.

The last volume of the catalogue marked the culmination of a remarkable quarter of a century in which Robert Latham, his co-editor of the diary, William Matthews, and a large team of contributors succeeded in producing both a masterly edition of the diary and a definitive description of Pepys's bequest to his college. The first volume of the diary had appeared while I was still at George Bell & Sons, and had been marked by an exhibition at the National Portrait Gallery in 1971 which I curated, commissioned by Roy Strong and designed by Julia Trevelyan Oman. After they married the following year, I received a card from Moscow, announcing that 'Mr and Mrs Pepys' were on honeymoon there.

The successful conclusion of both the editing of the *Diary* and the library catalogue had to be marked in a suitable fashion, and at the suggestion of Richard Luckett, the Pepys Librarian in succession to Robert Latham, the annual Pepys dinner at Magdalene, which had recently fallen into abeyance, was revived in Robert's honour, and hosted jointly by the College and Boydell & Brewer. It was a splendid occasion, and he was presented with a bottle of vintage wine from Château Haut Brion, chosen because on 10 April 1663, Pepys described tasting at the Royal Oak Tavern 'a sort of French wine called Ho Bryen, that had a good and most particular taste I ever met with'.

Original series completed 1994; supplementary series, latest volume (2004) Census of Printed Books by C. S. Knighton, ISBN 9781843840046, hardback, 297 mm x 210 mm, 400 pp, £110/$195

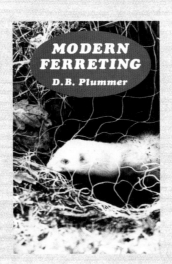

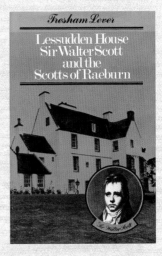

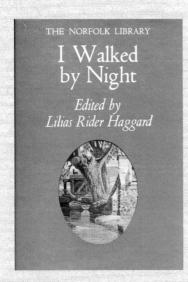

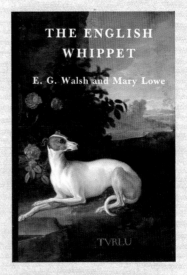

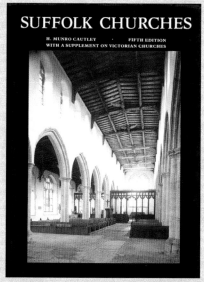

SUFFOLK CHURCHES

H. MUNRO CAUTLEY · FIFTH EDITION
WITH A SUPPLEMENT ON VICTORIAN CHURCHES

The
Medieval Book
and
A Modern
Collector

Essays in Honour of
Toshiyuki Takamiya

EDITED BY
Takami Matsuda
Richard A. Linenthal
John Scahill

TT

RECORDS OF THE MEDIEVAL SWORD

EWART OAKESHOTT

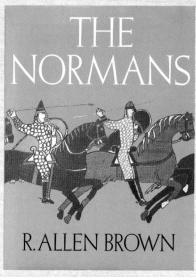

THE NORMANS

R. ALLEN BROWN

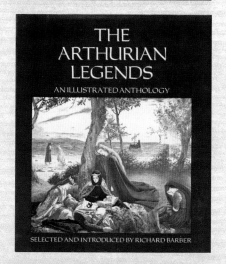

THE ARTHURIAN LEGENDS

AN ILLUSTRATED ANTHOLOGY

SELECTED AND INTRODUCED BY RICHARD BARBER

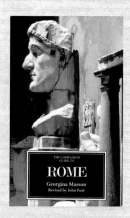

THE COMPANION
GUIDE TO
ROME
Georgina Masson
Revised by John Fort

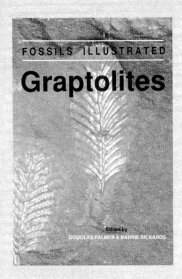

FOSSILS ILLUSTRATED

Graptolites

Edited by
DOUGLAS PALMER & BARRIE RICKARDS

The Age of
Sutton Hoo

Edited by
Martin Carver

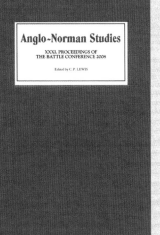

Anglo-Norman Studies

XXXI PROCEEDINGS OF
THE BATTLE CONFERENCE 2008

Edited by C. P. LEWIS

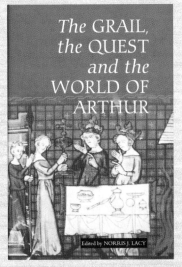

The GRAIL,
the QUEST
and the
WORLD OF
ARTHUR

Edited by NORRIS J. LACY

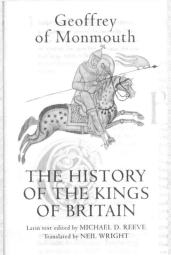

Geoffrey
of Monmouth

THE HISTORY
OF THE KINGS
OF BRITAIN

Latin text edited by MICHAEL D. REEVE
Translated by NEIL WRIGHT

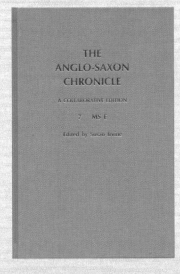

THE
ANGLO-SAXON
CHRONICLE

A COLLABORATIVE EDITION

7 MS E

Edited by Susan Irvine

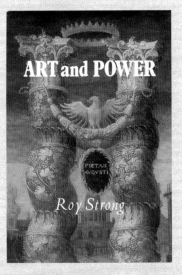

ART and POWER

PIETAS
AVGVSTI

Roy Strong

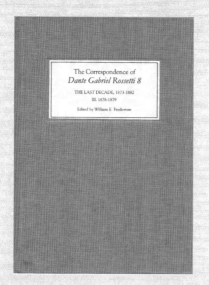

The Correspondence of
Dante Gabriel Rossetti 8

THE LAST DECADE, 1873–1882
III. 1878–1879

Edited by William E. Fredeman

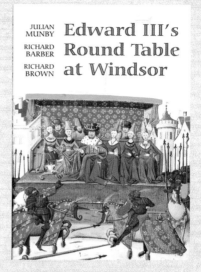

JULIAN MUNBY

RICHARD BARBER

RICHARD BROWN

Edward III's Round Table at Windsor

A Companion to the Fairy Tale

Edited by Hilda Ellis Davidson and Anna Chaudhri

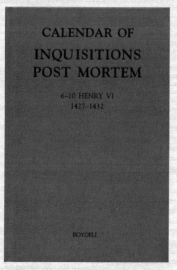

CALENDAR OF

INQUISITIONS
POST MORTEM

6–10 HENRY VI
1427–1432

BOYDELL

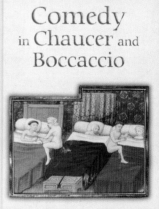

Comedy
in Chaucer and
Boccaccio

CAROL FALVO HEFFERNAN

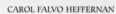

ROGER QUILTER
HIS LIFE AND MUSIC

VALERIE LANGFIELD

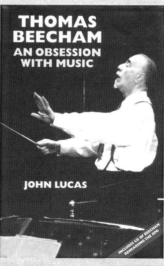

THOMAS
BEECHAM
AN OBSESSION
WITH MUSIC

JOHN LUCAS

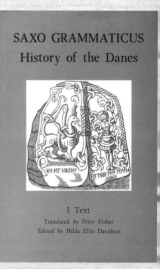

SAXO GRAMMATICUS
History of the Danes

I Text
Translated by Peter Fisher
Edited by Hilda Ellis Davidson

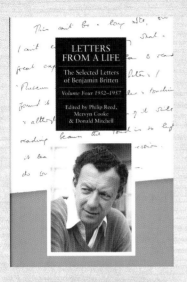

LETTERS
FROM A LIFE

The Selected Letters
of Benjamin Britten

Volume Four 1952–1957

Edited by Philip Reed,
Mervyn Cooke
& Donald Mitchell

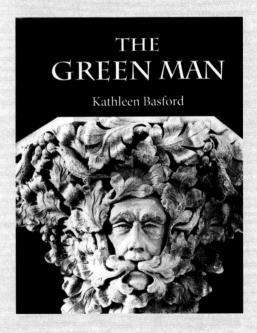

THE PARLIAMENT ROLLS
OF MEDIEVAL ENGLAND
1275–1504

V

EDWARD III · 1351–1377

THE DYING
AND THE DOCTORS

THE MEDICAL REVOLUTION IN
SEVENTEENTH-CENTURY ENGLAND

Ian Mortimer

STUDIES IN HISTORY

THE
GREEN MAN

Kathleen Basford

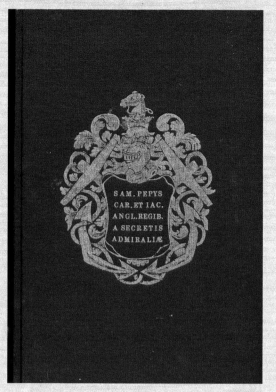

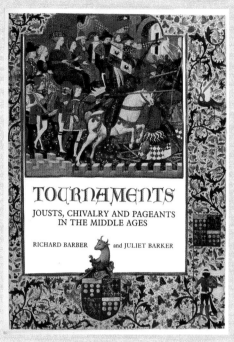

TOURNAMENTS

JOUSTS, CHIVALRY AND PAGEANTS
IN THE MIDDLE AGES

RICHARD BARBER and JULIET BARKER

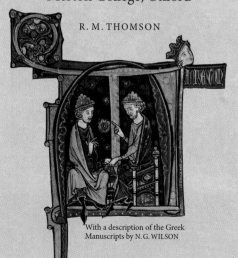

A Descriptive Catalogue of
the Medieval Manuscripts of
Merton College, Oxford

R. M. THOMSON

With a description of the Greek
Manuscripts by N. G. WILSON

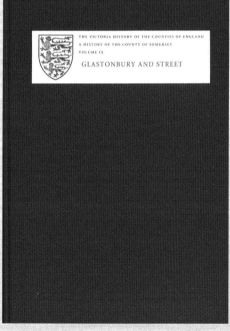

THE VICTORIA HISTORY OF THE COUNTIES OF ENGLAND

A HISTORY OF THE COUNTY OF SOMERSET

VOLUME IX

GLASTONBURY AND STREET

THE VERNON MANUSCRIPT

A FACSIMILE OF
BODLEIAN LIBRARY, OXFORD, MS. Eng. poet. a.1.

CHAUCER STUDIES

Medieval literature, 1979–

Chaucer Studies was the second major academic series from D. S. Brewer, following on from Arthurian Studies. It started with an unusual title, *Music in the Age of Chaucer*, with a companion volume of *Chaucer Songs*, which fitted Chaucer's texts to contemporary French music.[29] More typical was the third volume in the series, a collection of essays on Troilus and Criseyde. The series now runs to forty volumes, and most of today's distinguished Chaucer scholars have published an essay or a monograph in it.

It was the precursor of a number of literary series, such as *Studies in Medieval Romance*, and series publishing has always been a major part of our activities. I hope we have avoided the danger of simply adding titles because they fit the parameters of the series; ideally any title in a series should be capable of standing alone, but it is not always easy to keep rigorously to this standard.

Chaucer Studies was inspired by Derek Brewer's own work, and he was the effective editor of it, although his name never appeared formally on the books. A reissue of his own *Chaucer and his World* appeared outside the series; it had originally been published by George Rainbird, and he used to refer to it as his 'Chaucer novel'. It is a brilliant evocation of Chaucer and his times, with just the right judicious mixture of speculation and fact to bring that world to life. Our other Chaucerian activities ranged from collaboration with the Pilgrim Press on the Chaucer variorum edition, the production of Chaucer facsimiles (see *Troilus and Criseyde*) and even putting a blue plaque on the site of the house in Ipswich where Chaucer's family kept a tavern.

Latest title: Comedy in Chaucer by Carol Falvo Heffernan, ISBN 9781843842019, 168 pp, £45/$90

---

[29] Use of the same tune for multiple texts was a commonplace of early medieval music.

COMPANION GUIDE TO ROME

Georgina Masson
Revised by John Fort

Travel, 1998

The Companion Guides were started by Vincent Cronin in 1963 and published by Collins for many years. They acquired an excellent reputation, but changing patterns of travel meant that by 1995 they were proving difficult to publish; the old-style touring by car, which made titles such as the *Companion Guide to the West Highlands* so successful in their day, was being replaced by holidays focused on one centre. When we bought the series, it had already been sold to one publisher who had failed to make it work (and failed to pay for it). It was perhaps, in the context of our list, a mistake, but by slimming down the list to concentrate on cities, it has produced steady sales over the years. The jewel in the crown was the *Companion Guide to Rome* by Georgina Masson, which was badly in need of revision, as the author had died in 1980. The process was a very difficult one, because it was a classic text, and we had to preserve the original as far as possible, while making sure it was accurate and up to date. Through Eve Borsook, author of the *Companion Guide to Florence*, we enlisted the help of Ornella Francisci Orsini, who had worked with the conservation society *Italia nostra*, only to have a fax from her saying that having read three chapters she thought the book was terrible. Fortunately, after another three chapters she decided that she was enthusiastic about the project. A few loose ends remained to be tied up when she had finished; Helen and I flew to Rome and explored museums which were about to reopen with the help of an introduction from Signora Francisci Orsini, and a pocket torch, since the lighting was not yet installed. On the flight back, we noticed a couple with a copy of the by now rare earlier edition, and caught up with them at the baggage claim. It turned out that they had known Georgina Masson, and one of them had walked her dog when he was a boy. They were enthusiastic about the reissue and the idea of a launch party in Rome. Boydell had an excellent representative in Italy at the time, and she duly sent out invitations to the event, at a local bookshop, marked RSVP. Ten days before the party, she rang to say that she had had one reply, from the British Ambassador, and that Monsignor Burns from the Vatican Archives wanted to make a speech lasting half an hour; would we kindly come out and offer moral support at what promised to be a problematic occasion? A message went to Monsignor Burns that he could have ten minutes, and we went rather dubiously to Rome. When Helen and I got to the bookshop, there seemed to be some kind of demonstration going on: the street was full of people. Fortunately, it turned out that they were all trying to get into the bookshop, and that RSVP meant nothing to Italians – they had simply turned out in force. Charles Burns, an Irishman of great charm and total recall, who had known Georgina Masson and everyone else of note among her contemporaries, spoke for forty-five minutes, but it was all a great success. The book is now in its ninth edition, ably and regularly updated by John Fort, and is about to appear with new maps.

ISBN 9781900639453, 181 x 108 mm, 704 pp, 32 illustrations, 29 maps, £16.99/$34.95

A COMPANION TO THE FAIRY TALE

Edited by Hilda Ellis Davidson and Anna Chaudhuri

Literature and folklore, 2003

Over the last decade, the word *Companion* has appeared in the title of more than sixty books on the lists published across the Boydell & Brewer group. They have been particularly prominent in the Camden House and Tamesis lists, briefly described at the end of this book, and indeed the first such volume was in 1998, published by Camden House. It is often a format used for undergraduate course volumes, but we have always aimed at a higher academic level, and to present the current research and thinking on a subject for both specialists in the topic concerned, and scholars who may want a quick overview because their own research touches on that topic.

Many of the titles are obvious choices, but it is often the more eclectic ones that are the most enjoyable: the wide-ranging *Companion to Magical Realism* which Tamesis published comes to mind, and *A Companion to the Fairy Tale*, edited by Hilda Ellis Davidson and Anna Chaudhri. This arose from a particular enthusiasm on the part of Derek Brewer, whose essay on 'The Interpretation of Fairy Tales' opens the volume. It was a field in which we had been active before: for a number of years we had published for the Folklore Society, one of those splendid Victorian foundations which, after a period in the doldrums, has found renewed life in the last fifty years.

Folklore is treated much more seriously, as a branch of anthropology, in the United States. When I first encountered the Folklore Society in the early 1970s, the committee was rather maliciously described to me as a 'coven of witches', but under Hilda Ellis Davidson's energetic leadership it became a forum for solid scholarship in an area which, relying as it so often does on elusive word of mouth testimony, can succumb to personal enthusiasms rather than genuine research. Derek was also very interested in the psychological element in fairy tales. We occasionally published books which we felt might be wrong or flawed, but which might start a useful debate because they looked at a subject from a different viewpoint, such as John Darrah's *Paganism in Arthurian Romance* and Anne Wilson's *Traditional Romance and Tale*. Both received mixed reviews, but the latter spurred Derek on to produce his own *Symbolic Stories*, which covered some of the same ground.

ISBN 9781843840817, paperback, 304 pp, £19.99/$37.95

THE CORRESPONDENCE OF DANTE GABRIEL ROSSETTI

Edited by W. B. Fredeman

Art history and literature, 2002

The Correspondence of Dante Gabriel Rossetti had a rather unusual origin; bad notices do not usually lead to anything more than some discomfort on the part of the author or editor. Here, the effect of a bad review was a rather different story. As William Fredeman, the editor, explained in his introduction, it was 'launched as a result of a pair of "Mack the Knife" reviews', by him, of an earlier edition which had no index and many editorial failings. The Clarendon Press, which had published it, invited him to do a new edition; as he worked on it he discovered that the original edition constituted 'an editorial nightmare, containing every possible kind of error save forgeries'. Not only did he have to start again from the beginning, but he had to contend with the change from typewriter to computer and with two changes of publisher. After Clarendon abandoned it on grounds of cost, it was taken over by Chadwyck-Healey Ltd. The first volume had been typeset at the time of Fredeman's death, but by then Chadwyck-Healey was in the process of being taken over. Since this was almost the only book on their list – their main business being microfilms and electronic databases – the new owners were not anxious to take it on, and Charles Chadwyck-Healey asked us if we would step in. The first two volumes appeared in 2002, six further volumes have since been published, and the last text volume should be ready next year, an average of one volume a year.

Latest volume: The Correspondence of Dante Gabriel Rossetti 8, ISBN 9781843841319, 244 x 172 mm, hardback, 434 pp, colour frontispiece £125/$250

COUNTRY DOCTOR

Geoffrey Barber

Local history, 1975

Local publishing was the mainstay of Boydell's early years, and to give the list some kind of identity and coherence, we started three series for East Anglia, *Norfolk Library*, *Suffolk Library*, and *Essex Library*. These were a mixture of reprints and new books; Norfolk was the most productive county, with *I Walked by Night* and *Rabbitskin Cap*, both edited by Lilias Rider Haggard, the daughter of H. Rider Haggard, and Adrian Bell's collections of articles, *The Green Bond* and *A Countryman's Notebook*.

   The series embraced forgotten classics, a number of sporting books, and the occasional new title. One of these was by my father. When he retired in 1967 he wrote about his early days as a doctor in general practice in a series of articles for a medical magazine called *Update*. When these came to an end, I suggested that he might put these together as a book, and the result was *Country Doctor*. It was a great success, if a very local one: we must have sold over a thousand copies through one bookshop in Dunmow in north Essex, where he had worked all his life. But it also achieved a wider audience because he had been involved in the foundation of the Royal College of General Practitioners, and general practice was beginning to be regarded as a distinctive medical speciality. In his day, it was something that you might choose to do after hospital training; and he had never really intended to take it up. However, there was a tradition that when a doctor retired and wished to sell his practice, he offered it to his old hospital. Someone would come down and look at it, and report back to his fellow-trainees to see if they were interested. My father arrived in Dunmow to find that the retiring doctor was convinced that he had come to buy the practice, and my father claimed that he did not want to disillusion him; he had really intended to be a surgeon, but this changed the course of his career. He painted a wonderful picture of a world which had altered out of all recognition between 1929 and his retirement nearly forty years later, and Helen and I have encountered a number of unexpected people who have read and enjoyed it, including a doctor whom we met over breakfast in a B & B in Rochester, NY.

Out of print

A DESCRIPTIVE CATALOGUE OF THE MANUSCRIPTS OF MERTON COLLEGE, OXFORD

R. M. Thomson

Manuscript studies, 2009

This is the fourth manuscript catalogue which Rod Thomson has produced under the D. S. Brewer imprint. He is the leading expert in the field, a distinctive achievement for someone whose base is in Tasmania, and his previous three catalogues were for cathedral libraries – Lincoln, Hereford and Worcester. He first published with us through the Suffolk Records Society on the archives of Bury St Edmunds Abbey, and, suitably for someone specialising in ecclesiastical repositories, he is also a fine organist. In 2001 he gave a recital for us on the famous seventeenth-century organ at Framlingham. Playing the cathedral organ is one perk of his labours, but on his first project, at Lincoln, he found himself in a situation worthy of a Trollope novel. The chapter was divided by a row over the exhibition of the Lincoln copy of Magna Carta in Australia, which had been intended to raise money, but had cost more than it brought in. The two sides were not on speaking terms, but Rod, as a neutral outsider living in the chapter close, was the confidant for both sides; he said it was like living in one of the Barchester novels. Hereford was a much less problematic experience, though we had difficulties with the colour reproduction of the plates. I had to go and check them against the originals, working in the chained library which is open to the nave of the cathedral in the clerestory. Unfortunately, this meant that there was a good deal of dust around, and the nearest washbasin was across the cloisters and down a steep spiral staircase, which meant much coming and going to avoid marking the manuscripts. But the results, as with all Rod's volumes, were splendid.

He moved on to his first college library, at Merton, but did not leave the ecclesiastical world, because it contains more sermons than any of the cathedral libraries; and analysing sermon collections is perhaps the most demanding exercise that a cataloguer of medieval manuscripts can undertake. His current project, at Corpus Christi College, Oxford, is fortunately very different, a largely secular and wide-ranging collection.

ISBN 9781843841883, hardback, 440 pages, 51 colour illustrations, 107 black and white illustrations, £95/$180

EDWARD III'S ROUND TABLE AT WINDSOR

Julian Munby, Richard Barber, Richard Brown, with Tim Tatton-Brown

Medieval history and archaeology, 2007

In August 2006, the year of the Queen's eightieth birthday, *Time Team* was given permission to dig at three of the royal palaces. At Windsor, two sites were investigated, one of which was the Upper Ward, outside the Queen's private apartments. The Bank Holiday weekend was set aside for digging and for the replacement of the lawn, so this was in effect a rescue dig, and one which was unlikely to be repeated. The particular object of interest was the possibility that the great 'house of the round table', mentioned in accounts and in a chronicle of the late fourteenth century, might be found, even though it was never completed. I was sceptical about the existence of anything as large as the two hundred foot diameter structure specified in the chronicle, but a geophysical survey a week or two before the excavations started showed a huge shadow across the lawn, which measured just under two hundred feet. The existence of the House of the Round Table was proved by the discovery of the remains of the foundations, around which were scattered fragments of the stones which the accounts told us had been used in the building.

Television work, unless you are a technician or one of the presenters, is largely a matter of hanging around. I was one of four medievalists present and we whiled away the time by discussing all the evidence we could amass about Edward's Round Table. I suggested that Boydell might publish this, and an outline was agreed and accepted. The text was written and researched by the end of January, and the necessary photos obtained. We were also able to include the full archaeological report, Latin transcripts of the accounts, and an English translation of these and all the chronicles which referred to the occasion. The whole book was typeset and ready for the printer within six months of the end of the excavations, and was published in May 2007.

ISBN 9781843833130 (hardback), 312 pp, 16 colour and 17 black and white illustrations, 10 diagrams, £40/$80
ISBN 9781843833918 (paperback), £14.99/$27.95

THE ENGLISH WHIPPET

E. G. Walsh and Mary Lowe

Sporting books, 1984

An offshoot of the field sports books which we published in the 1970s was an informal series of titles on individual dog breeds. The world of pedigree dog breeding and the intense enthusiasm of owners and breeders were unlike anything we had encountered before. We came at it from a slightly unusual angle: there was already a massive business centred on handbooks for the popular breeds, and although we carried some of these titles, they were distributed on behalf of American and German publishers. We found that there was a market for books on highly unusual breeds such as the mastiff and bull-mastiff, which clearly included many people who were intrigued by the dogs but could not afford to own them: we calculated that we sold more copies of the mastiff book than the total number of mastiffs worldwide. Titles such as *The Clumber Spaniel* and *The Flat-coated Retriever* were the only books available on the subject, and *The Complete Jack Russell Terrier* sold very well in the United States even though the breed was almost unknown there.[30] The most elegant of the breed books was *The English Whippet*, by Ted Walsh and Mary Lowe. Mary said of her fellow author that a walk with him was never without incident, because he would always lob something into the brambles to see what came out. Ted was an expert on lurchers, and had written *Lurchers and Longdogs* for us. Mary's connections with the art world and their mutual enthusiasm for the visual history of the breed meant that the book began with a history of the whippet and its predecessors in the paintings of the eighteenth century, and it was certainly the best-written of these often all too practical titles.

When Ted Walsh died, the funeral notice said, after the usual details, 'Longdogs welcome.'

Out of print

---

[30] An old friend from Cambridge days had moved there, and his wife had taken Jack Russells with her; a local breeder became enthusiastic about them, and imported the books as the Jack Russells established themselves in America.

FROM CUCHULAINN TO GAWAIN

Elisabeth Brewer

Medieval literature, 1973

It was something of a miracle that the firm of D. S. Brewer survived the publication of the first two books under its imprint, *From Cuchulainn to Gawain* and *Medieval Comic Tales*, by Elisabeth and Derek Brewer respectively. I say survived because, although the books themselves were all that could be expected, the problem was that they were produced by Cambridge University Library's printing unit, and the proofs contained more misprints than even the most slapdash academic products of today – largely because the primitive computer setting of the period meant that every time the proofs were corrected, a raft of new errors was introduced. We eventually managed to get the setting to a respectable, though not perfect, state, and issued the books at the princely sum of £2.95 hardback and £1.25 in paperback. *From Cuchulainn to Gawain* was reissued in 1992 under a new, more literal title. The original title was one of those 'literary' phrases which sound good (particularly to authors) but which do not describe the book. In this case, the wording was not clear rather than totally obscure: we have battled against this kind of title – particularly quotations! – for many years, but in our early days we had not realised how it could work against us when selling the book to libraries.

New edition: *Sir Gawain and the Green Knight: Sources and Analogues*, ISBN 9780859910040, 192 pp, £14.99/$27.95

GRAPTOLITES

Barrie Rickards

Palaeontology, 2001

Derek Brewer's contributions to the Boydell & Brewer catalogue were far from being confined to his specialist subjects. He also brought to us a series on fossils, and a list of fishing books. Both of these originated in conversations while he was out jogging with a Fellow of Emmanuel College (of which he was Master), Barrie Rickards. Barrie, who taught geology, had long been interested in the idea of producing a high-quality photographic series illustrating fossils; he complained that the standard textbooks placed thumbnail photos in the margins, and that these were worse than useless, in many instances, for identifying a particular specimen. It was a challenge, as really high quality reproduction in black and white was essential; but the photographs were superb, and the first volume, on *Graptolites*, has some marvellous abstract images. Black and white photography, with its emphasis on contrast rather than colour gradation, outlines the fossils and their structures wonderfully. The illustrations were accompanied by an authoritative text, and three volumes appeared in all: but they were time-consuming to produce and demanded an available corpus of photographs to the required very high standard. Sadly the series petered out because the necessary material was not readily available.

Barrie's other enthusiasm, fishing, was a subject on which we knew as little as we did about geology. His real passion was fishing for pike and its relation the zander, and he would do this on his geological expeditions. He was once in the Arctic on such an expedition, when a Soviet army helicopter landed to see what they were doing. When he explained, they said that they knew a much better place fifty miles away. Barrie said he had no means of getting there easily, whereupon they took him and his colleague in the helicopter.

Of the five books he did for us, *Angling: the Fundamental Principles* was the most ambitious, an attempt to write a kind of *Compleat Angler* for today, with a strong input from his scientific training. It was very successful, but the list moved on from the country and sporting books.[31]
Out of print

---

[31]   In the end the entire list was sold on to another, rather short-lived, publisher.

THE GREEN MAN

Kathleen Basford

Art history and folklore, 1978

When Kathleen Basford came to us in 1976 with her extraordinary collection of photographs of the Green Man, from whose head leaves sprout, found in classical and medieval sculpture and art, we were very doubtful whether it could be successfully published. There were over 150 images, on a subject which was little more than a footnote in folklore studies, and which was more usually treated as part of architectural ornament. From this collection she had conjured a highly personal quest for the Green Man, based on wide reading and sound scholarship; her researches had turned up Green Men as far afield as Iraq and Lebanon, and as early as the second century AD, before it became a frequent image in Gothic art in England, France and Germany. We hesitantly printed a small number of books, which sold fairly rapidly. Even so, our then sales manager opposed the idea of a reprint, but the Green Man was very much in tune with the mode of the times and on taking over the sales department a year or two later, Ian Stevens put in hand a successful reprint. The book had been printed by letterpress, and when the printer closed, the original blocks were lost; we had to reprint by litho, at considerable extra expense, but the litho printer also closed. With the generous help of the charity Common Ground[32] to whom Kathleen Basford had given the original photographs, we recreated the book once more, and it is now in its fifth printing.

Another similarly unexpected title from the same period was Stella Newton's *Fashion in the Age of the Black Prince*. Stella Newton had started her career as an apprentice to a Bond Street couturier, and moved into designing for the theatre: she had designed the costumes for the first performances of T.S. Eliot's *Murder in the Cathedral*. She later worked at the Courtauld Institute, specialising in dating paintings by the fashions depicted by the artists. *Fashion in the Age of the Black Prince* was a pioneering work, because she had used the royal accounts of the time, as well as contemporary manuscript miniatures, to build up an intriguing picture of the fashionable trends of the mid fourteenth

---

[32] As its declared objective is to link the arts and the environment, *The Green Man* is an entirely appropriate cause for it to support.

century. We took it on with some hesitation because it seemed such an unexpected subject, but both academics and 're-enactors' loved it, and it has sold over 4000 copies so far.

The Green Man: ISBN 9780859914970, paperback, 276 x 216 cm, 128 pp, 170 black and white illustrations, 3 line illustrations, £20/$37.95

Fashion in the Age of the Black Prince: ISBN 9780851157672, paperback, 276 x 216 cm, 160 pp, 52 illustrations, £19.99/$37.95

HISTORIA REGUM BRITANNIE

Geoffrey of Monmouth

Arthurian literature, 1985–2007

The Vinaver Fund[33] has been a generous patron of Arthurian studies for the last thirty years, and Boydell & Brewer have published many works with their assistance. Our involvement, however, goes rather deeper than that, in that I and our chairman, Sam Wilson, helped to set up the fund as a charitable trust. It was a curious story. In the early 1970s, an American firm which made commemorative china approached the International Arthurian Society to ask them to put their imprimatur on a set of Arthurian plates. The committee of the International Society refused to do this on scholarly grounds; but the treasurer, Cedric Pickford, persuaded the British branch, as an independent if somewhat nebulous organisation, to become the official sponsors of the plates in return for a modest royalty on each set sold. He saw this as a small contribution to the branch's expenses; the contract was signed, and nothing more was thought of it until the first cheque, for over £25,000, arrived. This was far more than an organisation whose bank balance was in three figures could handle, and at the annual meeting of the Branch, the question of how to set up a charitable trust was mooted. I knew that Sam Wilson had some experience in this field as a solicitor, and offered to ring him the next morning, since the branch would not meet again for another year, and get the necessary draft resolution and it was now late on Saturday night. So at 9 a.m. I rang him, and got a very sleepy response – he had been at a hunt ball until 4 o'clock, and I was not popular! However, he rose to the occasion, a resolution was passed, and in due course the Trust was established.

The first major project the Trust undertook was a massive one: there had long been a need for a proper edition of Geoffrey of Monmouth's *History of the Kings of Britain*, the origin of the medieval and modern versions of the Arthurian legend. It was a formidable task, for the text existed in over two hundred and fifty manuscript copies. Sorting out a master text meant collecting microfilms of all of them and working out the relationships between the manuscripts. Neil Wright, then a research student at Cambridge, was engaged

---

[33] Named after Eugène Vinaver, the editor of the manuscript of Malory's *Morte Darthur* found at Winchester in 1947.

to do this. Boydell both employed him on behalf of the Trust and gathered in the microfilms.[34] Four volumes appeared – a single-manuscript text for each of the two main versions of the text, a catalogue of all the manuscripts, and two ancillary studies – before it was clear that the cost of employing a full-time researcher was more than the fund could afford.

However, twenty years later, Professor Michael Reeve was able to produce a highly acclaimed text based on an analysis of key passages of each manuscript, with a translation by Neil Wright, which now provides the edition which has so long been needed.

History of the Kings of Britain, ISBN 9781843834410, 392 pp, £25/$47.95

---

[34] Fortunately we were able to get about half of the microfilms from a previous abortive attempt to prepare an edition, but several recently discovered manuscripts were in eastern Europe, and were obtained only with difficulty.

I WALKED BY NIGHT

'The King of the Norfolk Poachers'

Sporting books, 1974

Local books sold well in the early days of the company, and booksellers would often suggest titles to be reprinted. Tom Cook, of the College Gateway Bookshop in Ipswich[35] not only did this, but also became a shareholder in the company. It was John Prime at King's Lynn who proposed *I Walked by Night*, a book with an underground reputation among poachers.[36] In the 1930s, Lilias Rider Haggard had been sent a manuscript by a local man, who called himself 'King of the Norfolk Poachers', about his exploits. It was written in his own idiosyncratic spelling, but she realised its potential, and edited it while keeping its original flavour. There is still a document in our archives by which Frederick Rolfe, the author, makes over the copyright to Lilias Rider Haggard for what was then the princely sum of £50. It is all in correct form; not for nothing was she the daughter of a man who had been a barrister before he wrote *King Solomon's Mines*.

Published before the Second World War with drawings by Edward Seago, it had been through six or seven printings, and now, according to John Prime, it had become hard to get hold of. It had been privately reprinted by Lilias Rider Haggard's nephew, Mark Cheyne, and when we approached him he was delighted to be relieved of the work of getting it printed in return for a good royalty. He too became one of our shareholders, and the book went on to notch up ten further printings, as well as a paperback edition for which we sold the rights to Oxford University Press.   *Out of print*

---

[35] A wonderful shop with a great reputation. One day a leading London book dealer drove up in his Rolls-Royce, and walked in unannounced. Tom Cook showed him the ground floor, whereupon he offered to buy the entire stock. Tom agreed, and the story goes (rather improbably) that it was loaded into the car. The dealer departed, satisfied, not realising that the cream of the stock was upstairs. Tom himself collected the Cuala Press editions of W. B. Yeats's work, which he would show to favoured customers. Tony Cox carries on the tradition, specialising in magnificent private press books and books about printing.
[36] Tom Cook warmly supported the reprint; he claimed he always knew when a poacher came into the shop wanting a copy, because they looked so ill at ease in a bookshop.

JOURNALS OF CAPTAIN COOK

Edited by J. C. Beaglehole

Maritime history, 1999

The Journals of Captain Cook, edited by J. C. Beaglehole, appeared under the imprint of the Hakluyt Society between 1955 and 1973. It is famous as a monumental work of scholarship, but it is also a highly complex set of volumes, because it includes over a hundred illustrations by the artists who accompanied Cook, and many maps, often in the form of fold-outs, as well as a portfolio of charts. We were the distributors for the Hakluyt Society at the time, and we always looked at the lists of the learned societies which we handled for possible reprints for a more general market. This, however, was on a different scale, and it was only with the support of Hordern House in Australia that we were able to undertake the huge job of reprinting, which involved going back to the original photographs and finding a binder who could handle all the manual work involved in mounting and folding the illustrations. It was a major addition to our list, and pointed the way forward to our involvement in maritime history; another lead title in this area was *Nelson's New Letters*, edited by Colin White in 2005.

With the advent of new short run printing technology and now with print on demand systems, we have tried to make available back volumes of learned societies, the most notable success being the retrieval of the backlist of the Early English Text Society. This had originally been reprinted by H. P. Kraus in New York, using a form of photocopying; but the list had ended up in the hands of a journals dealer who was based on the Hudson River. The society were anxious to regain control of the list, and I went to see them to negotiate this. I found myself going over the Hudson on the Rip Van Winkle bridge, to an extraordinary warehouse which had once been a massive ice store, with hugely thick brick walls and small rooms. Here the relatively small stock of reprint volumes still available was held; and it was not difficult to persuade them to relinquish the rights in return for the right to buy anything we reissued for the society at an advantageous discount. The whole list, a central resource for early English literature, has now been available from Boydell & Brewer for over a decade.

Another problem with such reprints is that the originals can be very scarce; this is true of the Henry Bradshaw Society, whose early twentieth-century volumes were issued to subscribers only, with no additional copies for sale. Fortunately, new technology designed to digitise books without disbinding them or damaging them in any way – using a very delicate and accurate page-turning device – has come to our aid, and a pilot experiment with the London Library, whereby we borrow the books for a month and pay a fee for each title photographed, is now under way.

Out of print

LESUDDEN HOUSE AND
THE SCOTTS OF RAEBURN

Tresham Lever

Local history, 1971

The first book published by the Boydell Press was *Lesudden House and the Scotts of Raeburn* by Sir Tresham Lever, and it appeared in 1971. Sir Tresham was the author of several books on seventeenth- and eighteenth-century history, and was the owner of Lesudden House. The book was too specialised for his regular publishers, so he came to us and asked us to publish at his expense. This type of publishing had been our original business plan; we were looking primarily at the possibility of books sponsored by large organisations or firms, but were also prepared to take on saleable books funded by their authors. It was, I suppose, a form of vanity publishing, and there were one or two titles which got under the net in the early days because the author made an offer we could not refuse, even though we were dubious about the book. The best were genuine oddities, such as the eighty-seven year old Yorkshire writer Jos Rothery, who had been highly commended for his entry to the Hutchinson New Novelists competition, and then told he was too old to be a 'New Novelist'. The Yorkshire papers loved *Now Then, Tom*, about his native Salterhebble in the 1900s, and it quickly reprinted.

Browsing through the company's first review book, the sheer variety of the titles is striking: a biography of the minor Victorian poetess Jean Ingelow, a limited edition of *The Last of the Valerii* by Henry James, which I hand-set, printed on mould-made paper and with a frontispiece by Julia Trevelyan Oman, *Heraldic Sculpture and the Work of James Woodforde*, the poems of Tony Buzan, now a high-powered education consultant and proponent of 'mind-mapping', *A History of Printing Ink*, and the autobiography of a circus chaplain. The only hint of future directions was in the reprints of two of my own books, *Arthur of Albion* and *Henry Plantagenet* – and if anyone wants a copy of *The Last of the Valerii*, there are still one or two of the original hundred left.

Out of print

LETTERS FROM A LIFE: THE SELECTED LETTERS OF BENJAMIN BRITTEN

Edited by Philip Reed

Music, 2008

The association between the Britten–Pears Library and the Boydell Press began in 1985, with the publication of the first volume in the *Aldeburgh Studies in Music* series, edited by Paul Banks, then the head of the library. Eight volumes have followed, and the editorship has been passed on to each successive librarian. The most spectacular volume, however, was not part of the series, and was a facsimile of the original score of *Peter Grimes*. Britten had given this to the conductor Reginald Goodall. With the growing fame of the opera, Goodall presented it to the library, where it is one of its most treasured possessions. The facsimile presented considerable problems, as it was largely in pencil with red crayon annotations, and was very difficult to reproduce clearly. There was a companion volume of essays about the opera, which was later issued separately.

The publication of Britten's letters began in 1991, under the Faber & Faber imprint; they had been the publishers of his music, and it was a natural choice at the outset. However, by volume IV, there were increasing problems, partly because the American co-publisher was reluctant to commit to the necessary number of copies to make the sums work; and it was our good fortune to be in a position to take on the three final volumes. The first of these appeared in 2008, on time and on budget, and although it will take a great deal more energy and dedication on the part of the editors and ourselves, we hope to maintain the schedule and produce the final volume in the centenary year of Britten's birth, 2013.

A different Aldeburgh association, with Aldeburgh Music, has resulted in *The New Aldeburgh Anthology*, compiled by Ariane Bankes and Jonathan Reekie, which, like the first anthology of 1972, celebrates the spirit of the place in images and words. The contributors emphasise both continuity and change in its musical and artistic life , and evoke once again the magic of its surroundings.

Volume IV, ISBN 9781843833826, hardback, 664 pp, £45/$90

THE MEDIEVAL BOOK AND
A MODERN COLLECTOR

Essays in Honour of Toshiyuki Takamiya

Edited by Takami Matsuda, Richard A. Linenthal and John Scahill

Medieval literature and manuscript studies, 2004

Festschrifts, the collections of essays originally devised in late nineteenth-century Germany as a way of honouring retiring scholars, can be dismal compilations of almost unrelated essays. The worst examples run to two or three volumes of short pieces, with the loose connection that they are contributed by the friends and students of the dedicatee. All too often, valuable essays were lost in the quagmire of these books; Sir Geoffrey Elton used to buy all the historical festschrifts that he could find because libraries were often reluctant to acquire such ragbag anthologies, and important items became impossible to find.

We have always encouraged thematic festschrifts, with a pre-determined theme that seems worthwhile in its own right. This has not always succeeded, but some volumes have established themselves as serious contributions to the subject; *On Britten and Mahler*, in honour of the Britten scholar Donald Mitchell, reprinted twice. But the grandest of the festschrifts we have published is *Medieval Manuscripts and a Modern Collector*, in honour of Toshiyuki Takamiya. The typography was by Lida Kindersley and Dale Tomlinson, and it was lavishly illustrated in colour and black and white and printed handsomely by Cambridge University Press, with a blind-stamped binding and spine label. The three themes, often complementary, were Chaucer, Malory and the collecting of medieval manuscripts, and many of the studies concerned manuscripts in the exceptional collection which Professor Takamiya has formed since 1970.

An additional pleasure and satisfaction in publishing this handsome volume was its embodiment of the longstanding connection between Boydell & Brewer and Japan.

Out of print

MODERN FERRETING

Brian Plummer

Sporting books, 1977

I Walked by Night was much in demand from the sporting books fraternity, and one of the leading mail order booksellers in the field sent us a handwritten manuscript for our consideration. It was entitled *Modern Ferreting*, which, the author claimed, had taken him forty-eight hours to write. To our surprise, it was fluent and distinctive, and we signed on Brian Plummer, who was to prove a highly successful author. It was this book that led to the famous episode in which Richard Whiteley was bitten by a ferret, voted the most popular out-take by the audience of the long-running TV show 'It'll be all right on the night', and regularly re-screened.

Richard Whiteley was interviewing Brian for Yorkshire TV, and Brian had brought a ferret with him. Brian handed it to Richard, assuring him that they were perfectly friendly, whereupon the ferret plunged its teeth into Richard Whiteley's hand. Brian tried unsuccessfully to detach it, so a pair of large leather gloves appeared from the side of the screen and seized the ferret.

The book was published just as the vogue for *Watership Down*, with its cast of heroic rabbits, was at its height. When I proudly showed our latest list to Douglas Matthews, the librarian of the London Library – we had just started to include a few academic books which I hoped would be of interest – he leafed through it, stopped at the page about *Modern Ferreting* and said reflectively, 'Ah, I see, *Modern Ferreting* – the answer to *Watership Down*.' The London Book Fair took place the next day, and we rushed out stickers quoting this comment; our reps loved them, and we were still being asked for them ten years later.

Brian Plummer was a vivid raconteur, born in a Welsh mining village, and had an enthusiastic following. He wrote a series of books for us on subjects such as rat-hunting and poaching, and once challenged our sales director to go on a rat-hunt with him, which he did, and survived to tell the tale.

Out of print

THE NORMANS

R. Allen Brown

Medieval history, 1984

The Normans came to us in a way that is a salutary lesson for publishers. Allen Brown was a member of the Suffolk Records Society council, and at one of the meetings at which Allen was present, there was a discussion about the extent to which an author's text should be copyedited. At one point I remarked, knowing that he was writing a book on the Normans for Phaidon, that what someone had just proposed was rather as though Phaidon had taken it on themselves to alter his style – of which he was justifiably proud – in the process of copyediting. 'But that's just what they have done', he said, 'and they refused to change it back, so I took the book away.' Naturally, after the meeting, I asked if we could publish it, the condition being that we did not alter a single comma. He agreed, and thanked us in the preface for allowing, 'amongst other things, sentences of more than half-a-dozen words and paragraphs of more than three inches.' However, we now were faced with the task of doing the picture research, design and production for a major illustrated book. Often the places to be illustrated were not to be found, and the pictures had to come from Allen Brown's own collection. In one or two instances, we had to explain that although a twenty year old snapshot might be unique, that did not mean it was going to reproduce well. In the end it was a handsome volume, excellently printed in Italy. We secured an order for 25,000 copies from Book Club Associates, and offered it to the History Book Club in the US. We heard nothing, and enquiries led nowhere, until they cabled that it was a main choice, provided we could deliver 25,000 copies for them as well in eight weeks. We were just about to go to press, but, after a mad scramble to find additional paper, we managed it.

The back cover had a photograph of the author in full Norman armour, charging down the site of the battle of Hastings. Scurrilous rumours claimed that he had fallen off at the bottom of the hill – unlikely, since he had been a cavalry officer during the war.[37]

Out of print

---

[37]   When he gave his course of lectures at King's College London, he would use a cavalry sword instead of a pointer.

PARLIAMENT ROLLS OF MEDIEVAL ENGLAND

General editor: Chris Given-Wilson

Medieval history, 2005

This is the largest single project that we have undertaken, and it came in a roundabout way. The parliament rolls and the accompanying petitions presented in parliament are a central record of English constitutional history and of the medieval history of England, and although they had been printed in the eighteenth century, a modern edition was badly needed. A seven-year project, funded by the Leverhulme Trust, was completed in 2004, the intention being that it should appear on the internet and be available on CD. However, in the intervening years, Cambridge University Press had largely withdrawn from CD publications, and the electronic costs had overrun the original budget. They decided to withdraw from the project, and Peter Robinson, of Scholarly Digital Editions, who had prepared the electronic version, took it over. They came to us for distribution, and in the course of discussions with Aidan Lawes of The National Archives, which was the copyright holder of the text and translations, I suggested that it would be feasible to produce a small print edition. Peter Robinson created a program to output the files in TEX, a typesetting system designed for the transfer of electronic material to print, and we divided the result into sixteen quarto volumes. Ironically, it was Cambridge University Press who produced the books for us. Despite the four figure price of the set, and the presence of both a subscription website and a modestly priced CD, it sold out within twelve months, and we are still producing a small number each year by short run reprints.

ISBN 9781843831617, 16 volumes, 297x 210mm, £1950/$3850

RECORDS OF THE MEDIEVAL SWORD

Ewart Oakeshott

Arms and armour, 1991

The annual International Congress on Medieval Studies at Kalamazoo has always been one of the focal points of the year for Boydell & Brewer, bringing together over three thousand academics and a handful of medieval enthusiasts more interested in re-enactment than the subtleties of scholarly discourse. At one such gathering a few years ago, you could find medieval cooks at work alongside smiths forging swords, and there was an occasion when the University of Toronto brought a full-scale medieval siege engine. Conference participants were encouraged to heave the ropes which operated it, but the results were not spectacular until someone enlisted the local American football team; instead of travelling forty or fifty yards, the missile narrowly missed a jogger two pitches away — a dramatic illustration of its real capacity.

One of the best titles in the field of re-enactment was Ewart Oakeshott's *Records of the Medieval Sword*. Ewart was a freelance lecturer and largely self-taught expert who had classified the types of medieval sword in a way which is now generally accepted as standard. He was given a suit of armour by his uncle, the novelist Jeffery Farnol, and used to lecture in this until it fell off a luggage trolley in Grand Central Station. Over the years, he had photographed and made notes on most of the swords which he came across, often at auction, and these records made up his first book for us. Many of them were in the hands of private collectors, and hence difficult to trace, so this was a useful resource.

But Ewart was also no stranger to controversy; he claimed to have found the missing sword from the Black Prince's tomb in Canterbury Cathedral, in an antique shop in Dorchester, and more seriously, he believed that the sword which appears on the cover of his book was the state sword of Edward III. He failed to persuade the Victoria & Albert Museum to buy it, but when it went to a private collector in Germany, persuasive tests showed that it could well be a genuine artefact of the period. The museum had rejected it because it had certainly come from a notorious forger of medieval artefacts, who had left his collection to his home town in Italy; when this came to be catalogued, it was quickly apparent that everything in it seemed to be a forgery. Ewart argued that any forger of such skill would have had genuine pieces from which to work as well as his stock of forgeries. The debate is unresolved, but the sword-hilt is a marvellous jacket image.

Ewart lived with Sybil Marshall, well known for her work in adult education, in a splendid Georgian house in Ely. Sybil was in fact our original contact; she had offered us her wonderful memoir of a Fenland childhood, *The Silver New Nothing*, some years before, but it was in the days before memoirs were fashionable with the public, and we had reluctantly said no; but Kevin Crossley-Holland heard about it when he joined us, and persuaded us that it could be done. Sybil threw a wonderful party for the launch, with her 'Fen Tiger' relations on whom the book was based. She could not help writing; her letters, in an elegant italic hand, were pages long, and always delightful to read.

ISBN 9780851155661, 276mm x 219 mm, paperback, 320 pp, 381 black and white illustrations, 84 line illustrations, £30/$60

ROGER QUILTER

Valerie Langfield

Music, 2002

At the seaward end of the road past our original office in Alderton you will find the eccentricity of Bawdsey Manor, monument to the Victorian entrepreneur and stockbroker Sir Cuthbert Quilter, with its Tudor façade towards the estuary and a front entrance modelled on a whim after a French château he had seen on holiday. It stands on cliffs made of Pulhamite, one of those eclectic inventions of the Victorian age, a special cement which imitates rock. It was here that the composer Roger Quilter grew up. His opus 1 was *Four Songs of the Sea*, settings of his own poems, and dedicated to his mother. But although he seems to have loved Bawdsey Manor itself, he was uneasy with the life of a younger son in a conventional Edwardian country house and in the family stockbroking firm.

The story of his life as a musician was admirably described in Valerie Langfield's *Roger Quilter*, which we published in 2002. Later composers admired, but rarely imitated, him; he had only one student, Muriel Herbert, mother of the biographer Claire Tomalin. Many of the Quilter family still live round Bawdsey, and remember him as a friendly, slightly distant figure. But his music continues to be recorded, and when we launched the book, we put on a study day at Bawdsey Manor with David Wilson-Johnson and David Owen Norris leading a master class and giving a recital in the evening. Valerie Langfield, the author of the book, gave a talk on recordings of Quilter's music, and we played my grandfather's copies of the single-sided 78s of Quilter's most famous songs, sung by their mutual friend Gervase Elwes, on a gramophone of the type Quilter himself might have owned, comparing them with modern tapes and CDs. The records may have been given to my grandfather by Quilter himself, since in 1908 he was best man at my grandparents' wedding. David Wilson-Johnson's recital, partnered by David Owen Norris, was hugely enjoyable, ranging from the early songs drawing on Quilter's time in Frankfurt and the 'wonderfully politically incorrect' *Foreign Children*; the programme notes commented drily that 'this song is rarely performed because of its text'. The main emphasis was of course on the magnificent settings of Shakespeare and the early-seventeenth-century poets which are among the classics of English song.

ISBN 9780851158716, 400 pp, 33 black and white illustrations, CD, £45/$90

SAXO GRAMMATICUS: THE HISTORY OF THE DANES

Translated by Hilda Ellis Davidson and Peter Fisher

Medieval literature, 1979

The History of the Danes by the early thirteenth-century Danish writer Saxo Grammaticus is famous as the source for the story of Hamlet, but it is much more than that: an invaluable store of information about the pagan past of Scandinavia, as recorded in an era when parts of the Norse countries were newly converted, and pagan memories fresh in the mind. Saxo's original Latin is difficult, and much of what he says requires a commentary to make it comprehensible. We published Hilda Ellis Davidson and Peter Fisher's edition and translation in 1979, and it remains in print. Translations may be complex and expensive to do, but the results frequently have a long life, particularly when medieval chronicles are concerned. Over the years, titles such as *The History of the Albigensian Crusade* and *The Chronica Maiora of Thomas Walsingham* have been a staple of our history list.

In medieval literature, the range is equally wide. The largest translation project we have undertaken, accompanied by a facing edited text, is 'Arthurian Archives', edited by Norris Lacy. So far, sixteen volumes have appeared, covering French, German, Italian, Norse, Dutch and Latin Arthurian romances, many of them unavailable elsewhere. David Johnson and Geert Claassens' Dutch romances alone run to over 1500 pages. Other projects have been translations from the troubadours and of the French heroic epics.

Translating new books from other languages is an ever more expensive business, with royalties to be paid to the original publisher and a fee rather than a royalty to the translator. In the past, there has been government cultural funding for translation, but apart from the Netherlands and Norway, this has been drastically curtailed. In a time when publishers have to look to a quicker return on their investment, translations such as Ole Benedictow's large-scale work on the Black Death are increasingly difficult to justify; but the risk can be worthwhile when the hardback sells out quickly and the title settles down to a long life as an easily-reprinted paperback.

ISBN 9780859915021, 528 pp, paperback, £25/$47.95

STUDIES IN HISTORY

Founding editor: Geoffrey Elton

History, 1986–

It was a casual encounter on the steps of the Cambridge University Library that brought us the *Studies in History* series. Sir Geoffrey Elton was President of the Royal Historical Society, and had founded a series designed to publish first books by young scholars, which were to be rigorously mentored and edited as a way of training them for future work. Derek met him soon after the printer who had originally produced them had gone out of business: the deal had been an unusual one, because their main focus had been on producing city company reports, but as these tended to appear at certain times of the year, they had spare capacity at other times. Geoffrey persuaded them to produce the books at their own expense, and arranged for them to be sold direct to the academic world. Bookshops could buy them, but there was no promotion to the book trade or to library suppliers. They had produced over forty volumes at this point, and he was anxious to find a way of continuing the project. We took the series on, but we made it a normal publishing operation, and the series has flourished ever since, with 74 volumes in the original series and almost as many again in the new redesigned series which began in 1997.

The committee meetings for the series were notable for an efficiency which I mentally classified as Prussian, knowing nothing of Geoffrey Elton's background. They invariably began two or three minutes before the scheduled time, and ended at least ten minutes early; you only spoke if asked to do so by Geoffrey, and almost everyone fell in with this routine. It was only after his death that I discovered that he was indeed the grandson of a Prussian High Court judge, and when he came to England shortly before the Second World War, the family had adopted a very English surname.

The concept of mentoring a young academic to develop their doctorate into a book by drawing on the expertise of established writers is one which, in an ideal world, we as publishers should be developing. Pressures of time – the urgency for publication to secure either an initial appointment or tenure – and of resources have so far made this impractical, but the model of *Studies in History* is one which could, and should, be applied in other disciplines.

Latest title: The Dying and the Doctors: The Medical Revolution in Seventeenth-Century England by Ian Mortimer, ISBN 9780861933020, 232 pp, £50/$95

SUFFOLK CHURCHES

H. Munro Cautley

Local history, 1973

Suffolk Churches was the first major book which the Boydell Press acquired. It came to us through Felicity Cambridge, a friend who had inherited a small publishing and printing firm in Ipswich, the history of which went back to the 1730s. She had recently married, and did not want to continue the publishing business, so we took over the stock. It was transported in a Citroën estate car with self-levelling suspension, which was never quite the same afterwards: an early lesson in the fact that books are very heavy in relation to their volume. When the stock of *Suffolk Churches* ran out, we set about reprinting. It was a book which had never been a very economic proposition, written by the diocesan architect H. Munro Cautley in 1937, and priced originally at a guinea because that was all that the clergy, expected to be the chief buyers, could afford. It was lavishly illustrated with the author's photographs; and indeed it was rumoured that Cautley would order scaffolding to be put up so that he could carry out a routine inspection, when in fact he wanted to photograph the detail of a roof at close quarters. It was printed by letterpress for us at the long-established Ipswich firm of W. S. Cowell, in their day one of the finest printers in England, and particularly famous for their replica of George V's stamp collection, in which the precise shade of each stamp had to be faithfully reproduced. We added colour plates, photographed by A. F. Kersting, a skilled architectural photographer; but without Cautley's privileged access the operation was sometimes tricky. I went with Tony Kersting to Thornham Parva to help him photograph the wonderful retable, then unrestored; and we found that the fierce light from the east window above the retable was making it almost impossible to get a useable image, even with floodlights. Happily there was a builder's ladder and a sheet of black polythene outside, and an impromptu blackout was organised. We also commissioned supplementary material on the current state of the churches, on the lost churches of the county, and on the Victorian churches which Cautley had excluded.[38] It was a costly exercise to redo this substantial work, and I remember a sleepless night or two worrying whether our finances would stand it. Fortunately they did, and the new edition sold out successfully. *Out of print*

[38] The text was held in such respect by local historians that we were told that it would be unwise to attempt any kind of rewriting,; corrections had to be presented as a supplement .

THOMAS BEECHAM

John Lucas

Music, 2008

A biography of Sir Thomas Beecham was long overdue when John Lucas began work on his book, but before it was completed, the publisher who had commissioned it, John Murray, was taken over. The new owners were not particularly in sympathy – I almost said in tune – with the project, and it was snapped up by Bruce Phillips, our music list adviser. Bruce was music editor at Oxford University Press when they made the extraordinary decision to close the English operation and move the list to New York, hardly the place for publishing the many distinguished books on English music which had been one of the staples of their list. He came with unrivalled contacts in the music world, and brought a series of high profile books to us, which were perfect additions to the list. *Thomas Beecham* was one of these, and it even came with one of our best launch parties ever which, thanks to the generosity of John Murray himself, was held at his old headquarters at 7 Albemarle Street. It was a delight to be in such an inner sanctum of publishing tradition and among the guests were eminent names from the music world, welcoming the first biography of a man who had made such an impression on British music in the first half of the twentieth century. And of course the conversation turned now and then to stories about Beecham, both familiar and unfamiliar. The book itself is enlivened by a splendid CD of Beecham in rehearsal, with 'out-takes' which both illustrate his style of handling an orchestra and his legendary humour.

ISBN 978184383402, 416 pp, 40 black and white illustrations, CD, £25/$47.95

TOURNAMENTS

Richard Barber and Juliet Barker

Medieval history, 1989

It was perhaps inevitable that we should one day publish a book on tournaments. I had explored the subject in my book *The Knight and Chivalry*, which appeared the year after we started the Boydell Press, and I knew that it was territory which had been regarded as too frivolous by serious historians. It was fifteen years later that we were offered a thesis which Maurice Keen, the most distinguished historian of chivalry, had supervised, Juliet Barker's work on the tournament in England. Not long after this was published, I suggested that she and I might collaborate on a proper history of the tournament, since nothing of the kind using proper scholarly conventions existed. It needed to be heavily illustrated, because much of the evidence was visual, and hence would have to be a popular book. I wrote the chapters on the tournament in Europe and she concentrated on the tournament in England; but I would be hard put to it now to say exactly who wrote some of the more general passages.

We took a dummy to Frankfurt, and found ourselves the subject of a feature in *The Observer* by Jonathan Raban; what happened next is best told in his words:

> Boydell & Brewer of Woodbridge is a small firm with a good monopoly position in the field of medieval history. It's run by Richard Barber and Kevin Crossley-Holland, both of whom have plenty of experience of London-based general trade publishing (Crossley-Holland used to be editorial director of Gollancz). Their stand at Frankfurt was of the table-and-two-chairs variety – a bare perch with a handful of bookjackets blue-tacked to the walls.
>
> I asked if I could see their 'Frankfurt book,' and Crossley-Holland opened a large brown envelope, not unduly full of papers. A contents page. Some sample typeset text. A sheaf of coloured illustrations. The book, co-authored by Richard Barber, was to be about tournaments, and was as yet only part-written. The contents page, though, looked promising – tournaments were pan-European; quite unlike the parochial British sport of modern class warfare. The illustrations, with their liberal splashes of scarlet and gold, were ravishingly pretty. 'Tournaments' was obviously an International Book.
>
> I kept on seeing Barber and Crossley-Holland on the moving staircases,

riding to appointments. They were traversing the world, with Italy, Portugal and Spain just round the corner, America one floor down, and the whole of Scandinavia in the basement. Frankfurt had transformed Boydell & Brewer into a multinational for a week, and Barber and Crossley-Holland were doing exactly what Bertelsmann, Kluwer, Penguin and Si Newhouse try to achieve with their takeovers and mergers – steadily milking a book of its subsidiary rights until it turns into a healthy commercial proposition.

By the end of the fair we had sold it to Lord Weidenfeld's new venture in the US, Grove Weidenfeld, and to Compagnie Douze in France, run by Valerie Giscard d'Estaing, daughter of the former president. This gave us the challenge of producing our first international co-edition; we had hoped for a German edition at the same time, but this only materialised in a reduced format some years later.

To mark the occasion, the obvious thing to do was to hold a tournament. We found an ideal site, at Framlingham Castle, and engaged an experienced tournament team based in Kent. They hired horses there, which were driven up to Suffolk. When the horses emerged from the horseboxes, they were in a highly excitable state; one rider was almost thrown into the (very deep) dry moat, and only two horses out of four were declared to be fit to ride. One of the jousters had a brand-new helmet, which he had not used before; and when I enquired why he had to be led to the start of the lists and caught at the other end, I was told it was because his vizor did not match his line of vision, and he was virtually jousting blind. Such episodes were probably all too familiar to medieval jousters, and despite the hitches, it was a resounding success, televised on both BBC and ITV.

Out of print

THE VERNON MANUSCRIPT

Introduction by Ian Doyle

Manuscript studies, 1987

One of the treasures of the Bodleian Library is MS. Eng. Poet. A. 1, a shelfmark which leads to an extraordinary anthology of late medieval English poetry, known as the Vernon Manuscript, after the donor who gave it to the library in the seventeenth century. It is a huge volume, weighing over 22 kg, and measuring 544 x 393 mm. It contains a very substantial proportion of all the known poetry of the fourteenth and fifteenth century, and the contents list runs to 377 items. The size of the original means that access has to be restricted to all but a handful of scholars who have good reason to examine it, quite apart from the fact that its weight is such that two people are nowadays required to lift it.

The suggestion that we should do a facsimile came from Toshiyuki Takamiya, and our initial reaction was that this would be almost impossible. However, after some detailed work on the problems involved, we realised that by reducing the size of the original page by 8%, we could print it reasonably economically, and we managed to find a bookbinder who could still machine-sew a book-block of this enormous size. Photography was a problem, in that the standard library cameras were not built to photograph whole pages of huge dimensions, but fortunately the Bodleian had recently installed new equipment that appeared to be able to handle it. So we negotiated a contract with them, and announced a pre-publication price for the volume. Photography began, but there was an immediate setback, because the adjustable spring-mounting which supported the volume had not been designed for such a weight, and the camera had to be rebuilt by the manufacturers. This led to a substantial delay, and when we finally printed and bound the book, the costs, and the price, had risen substantially. Unfortunately, this put it beyond the purchasing limits of many library budgets, and we had our biggest single return ever from Blackwells. They had subscribed at the original price, and could not now sell it to these customers, because it was above the price level set by them for automatic supply.

However, it has almost sold out over the years; we still have a small stock of sheets, which now have to be hand-bound as the sewing machines have long since gone. A final touch was the list of contents, which was on a throw-out at the back of the book, so that it could be read while the volume was open. This needed to be on a paper which would stand continual folding and unfolding; our printer suggested a new plastic paper which ICI had introduced, and on which he had recently printed their calendar. Apparently when the next year's calendars were shipped to Africa, the story went that there was disappointment that they were not on plastic again, because the pages of the calendar were ideal for patching the roofs of thatched huts.

ISBN 9780859912006, 530mm x 345mm, hardback, 856 pp, 8 colour illustrations, 818 black and white illustrations, £450/$800

VICTORIA COUNTY HISTORY

2003 –

Over the years, we have specialised – not necessarily by design – in rescuing eminent projects which are in some kind of difficulty. In the case of the *Victoria County History*, whose history goes back to the late nineteenth century, the problem was that the firm distributing the back volumes was about to move premises, and had no room for a huge and slow-moving back stock. By the time we came on the scene, an unfortunate attempt to sell off the titles through a secondhand book dealer had created more difficulties than it solved, and the distributor's warehouse was due to close within a matter of weeks. It quickly became apparent that if we were to take over the backlist alone, it would not make commercial sense, and we therefore negotiated to take over both the backlist and the current and future volumes. The negotiations were convoluted, but we managed to come to an agreement in time to clear the warehouse. Because the books were not packed, and packing facilities were no longer available, we had to hire a local removal firm to deal with the physical handling of the stock. Some of the stock had been damaged, and the titles also had to be sorted as they were packed. It was a large-scale operation, and involved several large removal vans, which could only be partly loaded because of the weight of the books. We then had to find suitable extra warehousing, and this in the end was found in a disused quail-rearing barn deep in the Suffolk countryside. Security was not a problem, because no-one would ever have found the warehouse without prior knowledge of its existence.

The titles in production were then redesigned by the Victoria County History team based in the Institute of Historical Research. This was a painstaking process, as the volumes have a very complex makeup, and a long process of trial proofs had to be undertaken before the handsome new design was agreed. In addition, we have begun a series of short run reprints of out of print volumes. The series is more widely available than ever before, and is largely on line, but this seems to encourage rather than reduce the rate of sale.

Latest volume: A History of the County of York: East Riding, Volume VIII: East Buckrose: Sledmere and the Northern Wolds, hardback, 304mm x 208 mm, ISBN 9781904356134, 304 pp, 65 black and white illustrations, 30 line illustrations, £95/$180

OTHER IMPRINTS IN
THE BOYDELL & BREWER GROUP

TAMESIS

CAMDEN HOUSE

JAMES CURREY

THE UNIVERSITY OF ROCHESTER PRESS

TAMESIS BOOKS LTD

Publishing firms have their beginnings in all kinds of strange places, but Tamesis was definitely unusual. It was in the back of a taxi coming down London's Finchley Road that Professor John Varey of Westfield College, chatting with the Spanish poet and academic, German Bleiberg, had the idea of starting a small publishing company. It was to be dedicated entirely to Hispanic studies, in which both young and established Hispanists would publish monographs and editions. It was to be called Tamesis Books, 'Támesis' being the Spanish for the river Thames. Formed in 1963 in the UK, the company's official name is Tamesis Books Limited (with no accent), although the books published are referred to in Spanish as Colección Támesis.

Varey, a veteran of Bomber Command for whom the cut and thrust of college politics proved infinitely less bruising than his wartime activities, was encouraged in his venture by R. F. Cutler of the important London bookshop, Grant & Cutler, which took on distribution for the new enterprise. Over the years Frank Cutler provided not only business advice but, at a moment of crisis, financial support. That Tamesis still flourishes now, as an imprint of Boydell & Brewer, is of course John Varey's achievement, but without Cutler's backing that achievement might never have been.

The moment was well chosen. While he undoubtedly envisaged the enterprise as a secure outlet for the fruits of his own research in the Spanish theatrical archives, John Varey's plan was for a general academic language and literature imprint. There was nothing similar in existence in Britain, and British Hispanism had entered a 'Golden Age', with enormous camaraderie among the scholars teaching in the relatively new university departments. In 1955 the Association of Hispanists of Great Britain and Ireland (AHGBI) had been formed.

During the Franco years, those Spanish intellectuals and writers who had chosen to remain in Spain were not fully at liberty to carry out research in all areas, and a multitude of their colleagues who had fled the regime were scattered across Europe and the United States. There was a great need for a focal point for Spanish studies, and the first editorial committee of Tamesis comprised the most distinguished names in contemporary international Hispanism, a staggering array of talent. In 1975 the company received the Nieto Lopez Prize from the Real Academia Española 'as a mark of the important campaign in the cause of Spanish literature waged by Tamesis Books Limited'.

Something of the spirit of these times, and John Varey's participation in it, is to be found in an account of the celebrations of the twenty-first anniversary meeting of AHGBI in 1976:

> The committee ... voted impulsively but unanimously to devote a high proportion of the Association's life-savings to the purchase of the complimentary Rioja Gran Reserva which graced the formal dinner. No bottle survived the occasion. ... John Varey astonished and delighted us with his account of railway trains in Galdós.

Nigel Glendinning relates that it was impossible for those who collaborated with John to understand how he found the hours to give to Tamesis publications, while teaching, chairing major university committees and pursuing his own research interests, including the above-mentioned history of the Spanish railway network, and puppet theatre. John's wide range of contacts located worthwhile projects in Spain, the UK and the US, but Charles Davis, a collaborator since the 1980s, recalls a steady stream of unsolicited incoming manuscripts, their authors attracted by Varey's personal prestige; costs were kept down by printing in Valencia during the summer months when the presses were underused.[39] The star-studded editorial board was asked to do very little, the decisions largely being taken by John and Alan Deyermond. John personally carried out all the editorial and administrative tasks: the copy-editing, contact with printers, proof-reading, and accounts.

Another of John's achievements, not to be ignored in this context, was to respond to a request for advice from Derek Brewer when he was thinking of setting up a publishing company. When this was related to Michael Brewer, Derek's son, to illustrate Tamesis's greater longevity, he countered swiftly that Derek must have outperformed his mentor, given that the company is now called Boydell & Brewer, and not Boydell & Tamesis.

In 1987, for reasons of logistics, the Tamesis editorial committee

---

[39]   There was apparently a minimum print run of 1000 copies; in the early days one or two books succeeded in selling something approaching this number, but by 1995 there were real problems with overstocks. I remember sending two 40-ton lorries loaded with Tamesis titles to the pulp merchants in 1996-7, loaded with the accumulated overstocks. [RWB]

was reduced to a small London-based group. John Varey (general editor) was assisted by Alan Deyermond, Nigel Glendinning, Ralph Penny and Verity Smith, while Charles Davis, Stephen M. Hart and (until 1988) Sue Lewis were editorial assistants. The association of Alan, Charles and Stephen with the company continued until very recently, Alan advising on medieval literature, Charles the standard-bearer of Varey's series 'Fuentes para la historia del teatro en España' and Stephen acting as general editor; but sadly, Alan died while the present book was in preparation: a special tribute is due to him for his involvement with Tamesis since its inception, throughout his long career. His contribution to the imprint's success was incalculable, his generosity to young scholars unmatched, and his input to so many volumes often unsung but vital to their success.

In 1989 Richard Barber became a board member when Boydell & Brewer took over Tamesis distribution world-wide. Frank Cutler was also on the boards of both companies, maintaining the old connection. John was still eager to explore new possibilities, and soon afterwards started Editorial Támesis, which was to be the Spanish-language publishing subsidiary of Tamesis. He had been assured that government funding was available to firms who were based in Spain and published learned works in Spanish. However, when he had spent a great deal of time over the summer every year for five years pacing the corridors of the relevant ministry, it was clear that this was a case of jam tomorrow. Richard Barber does not remember a single grant coming through, and the only people who made any money were the expensive Madrid lawyer and accountant who prepared the annual papers required. Tamesis came fully under the Boydell & Brewer banner in 1995, four years before John Varey's death , when it was clear that it was not viable as an independent entity.

When the first history of Tamesis was written, to mark 25 years of existence, John Varey noted that the average life of a family publishing company was around 30 years. To avoid demise, he believed it essential that Tamesis continue to innovate, in terms of personnel, ideas and technology. This year the advisory board has been extended to include again a range of internationally respected academics who are bringing fresh inspiration to the development plans, while modern methods revolutionise production. Within the Boydell & Brewer fold, Tamesis looks forward to celebrating its half-century four years from now. I hope John Varey knows.

CAMDEN HOUSE INC

James Hardin, founding director

Camden House was founded in 1979 by two professors of German who saw a need for a publisher of specialized scholarly books that might not be attractive to most university presses. There had been much discussion from the mid 1970s among scholars at the University of South Carolina in departments of English, American, German, French, and comparative literature about the difficulties of finding reputable publishers, specifically university presses, for what we considered deserving manuscripts. Our own university press at that time was generally unreceptive to works of literary criticism. In due course, our frustrated group was incorporated under the title 'Carolina Academic Publications' but there was much heat and little fire. It was thought that one "big" manuscript might pave the way (through heavy sales!) for more specialized works. Little thought was given to technical matters, such as typesetting, printing, binding, distribution, and as little to acquisitions and copyediting. To say we did not understand the publishing business in any sense, technical or otherwise, would be an understatement. Thus, nothing came of the discussions and members of the group went back to their individual interests.

After consultation with helpful individuals at a number of university presses, James Hardin and Gunther Holst (University of South Carolina) took the daring step of founding a series in German. Using trade publications for the most part, they invited scholars to submit manuscripts in the field of German and Austrian literature, linguistics, and culture, having established a distinguished editorial board that functioned primarily as an acquisitions arm, and secondarily as an A-list of vetters.

From the very beginning, Camden House stressed, to the extent possible, publishing books written in a clear, jargon-free style. To this end numerous style sheets were produced over the years, some designated for authors, others for publishers, others for specialized series. Translations were welcomed, as were studies that treated major authors or broad, major topics Every manuscript was carefully vetted and edited. Some authors rejoiced at the attention, others, of course, were less enthusiastic. But we soldiered on without making an all-out attempt to establish a goal for the number of books published in a given year. As a result, the Camden House output was rather slim in the first five years, but beginning in the mid 1980s Hardin expanded the scope of the press and with the establishment of a number of distinct series, was able to commission numerous manuscripts with due dates several years out in some cases.

This bore fruit in the following years: by the end of the 1980s, Camden House typically brought out 20-25 books each year and was also publishing *The Goethe Yearbook* and other series. A new series, *Literary Criticism in Perspective*, was established in the following decade, and in time broadened to include American and British literature. The aim of this more specialized series was, and is, to elucidate the role of literary criticism over the years, to show how it is subject to varying vogues and philosophical or critical viewpoints, and how criticism itself is a mirror of changing taste and critical bias.

In the late 1980s Camden House increasingly sought out highly qualified scholars to write or edit commissioned works, especially in its Companion series. It was fortunate in locating and working with prominent Germanists who in the next two decades brought out *Companions* to the works of such canonical writers as Hartmann von Aue, Grimmelshausen, Lessing, Schiller, Kleist, Heine, Thomas Mann, Rilke, Canetti, Stefan George, Thomas Bernhard, Döblin, Kafka, Hofmannsthal, and Schnitzler. In addition, *Companions* to major works were commissioned and published, and included *Companions* to Goethe's *Faust I and II*, to the *Nibelungenlied*, to Gottfried von Strassburg's *Tristan*, and to Mann's *Magic Mountain*. Distinct periods in the history of German literature were treated in Companions to German Realism, and to German Expressionism.

Another important aspect of the German program included trans-lations of such key works as Grimmelshausen's *Simplicius Simplicissimus*, the first great German novel; Johann Beer's early comic novel *German Winter Nights*; and Goethe's *Wilhelm Meister's Theatrical Calling*, the neglected forerunner to the prototype of the Bildungsroman, *Wilhelm Meister's Apprenticeship*. Individually authored monographs on virtually every prominent German writer have appeared in the Camden House list, as well as numerous works on German film, theater, song, satire, holocaust literature, literature of the German Democratic Republic, and Austrian literature. In 1994 a major step was made when Camden House added James Walker to its program, a former student of Hardin, whose skills in German and general literary knowledge were immediately of immense benefit to the publishing house. He quickly learned every aspect of the publishing trade and meticulously tracked the progress of the 35–45 projects on the boards at any given time. Publishing is detail work, and it entails working well with people: Walker was and is superb in these and other areas.

In any case, as Camden House operations came more and more into the orbit of Boydell & Brewer, our production standards rose steadily. Camden House gained much through the experience of Boydell, and took on ever more ambitious projects. Of these, the *Camden House History of German Literature*, which appeared in ten volumes, is the most detailed and thorough treatment of German literature in English; it engaged the collaboration of Germanists from the US, the UK, Germany, Austria, and Australia. This is perhaps the most significant achievement to date of our house, and consolidated the position of Camden House as one of the leading publishers on German literature in the Anglophone world.

In recent years Camden House has branched out into American literature, extending its series *Literary Criticism in Perspective* in that area as well. Camden has also published works on Canadian literature, and in recent years has attracted scholars of German cinema, music, and cultural history.

In 1998 Camden House became an imprint of its long-time distributor, Boydell & Brewer, and has continued to bring out books in all the areas described above under the editorship of James Walker. James Hardin remains a consulting editor with Camden House.

JAMES CURREY

JAMES CURREY, FOUNDING DIRECTOR

George Orwell's doomed year of 1984 was hardly propitious for Clare and James Currey to start their own firm to publish academic books on Africa. When people said we were 'brave' we took them to mean 'foolish'. I had enjoyed seventeen expansive years publishing at Heinemann: over 250 titles in the African Writers Series as well as numerous books for schools and universities. However the Nigerian foreign exchanges had crashed in April 1982 leaving Heinemann Educational Books (HEB) with container-loads of books unpaid for. It was the beginning of what came to be called 'the book famine' in Africa. Oxford, Longman, Macmillan and Heinemann all cancelled contracts for the new wave of academic titles which were emerging from the expanding universities in Africa and the new African Studies courses round the world. I saw a gap in the market and calculated that we could make ends meet with sales in the rich world and that any sales in Africa would be a bonus. The United States was the biggest market and at HEB I had been co-publishing titles with the university presses of California, Indiana, Wisconsin and Ohio; their treasuries always paid on the nail. In 1984-5 the pound reached its lowest point against the dollar in the whole of the twentieth century. It was the best time to start an export-led company. All we had to do was to telex the US press the costs for the whole job including printing copies for Africa and our own warehouse stock, and they almost always accepted by return.

British Tyre & Rubber, who had just acquired the Heinemann Group, put in a slash-and-burn MD who thought that African Studies academic publishing was a self-indulgence. Redundancy pay would keep us going personally. With the help of a Canadian student, late at night I removed my four-drawer filing cabinet of future projects; the MD considered it waste paper for burning. He assigned all the contracts to me to save HEB the costs of cancellation. I worked out three months' notice by a heavy programme of lunching my loyal authors to persuade them to give a chance to an untried firm. The MD did not even bother to tell John Watson, the President of HEB Inc in New Hampshire, that they would not be getting any future academic titles to stoke up their expanding business. John Watson said 'If HEB in London cannot produce the books we need, then we'll take them from James Currey Publishers!' They rapidly became our biggest US customer – and they paid on time. We joined with another former Heinemann colleague, Ian Randle in Kingston, Jamaica, to import his adventurous Caribbean academic list. About ten years after we started I was taken into the University of California, Berkeley campus bookshop, and there near the Pacific were all our books with our imprint which had come on different routes via our co-publishers across America. The crowded shelves certainly gave a good impression of ours being the biggest African studies list in the world.

So, how to get academic books into 'book famine' Africa? A network of authors and co-publishers in Africa found ingenious ways of getting us paid in dollars and pounds and printed books. Authors were the most effective fund-raisers. After working for years up-country in an African country, scholars were concerned that people in that country could have access to their book. We would ask our co-publisher what price in local currency would make the book accessible. UN agencies in New York and Geneva and the Scandinavian and Dutch aid agencies responded to the practical opportunity of co-publishing. Walter Bgoya, who had started the publishing house of Mkuki na Nyota in Dar es Salaam, was endlessly inventive and willing to make his schemes work. He persuaded Tanzanian customs to put impounded books on auction. But they did not think books had much value so he had to bid for a joint lot of books and car parts; he may well have also made a profit on the car parts. After President Museveni liberated Kampala, our book *Uganda Now* was the only new book in the country thanks to the editor Holger Bernt Hansen, who later became head of the Danish aid agency. I arranged an accessible price in shillings with the co-publisher, Uganda Bookshop. Traders quickly saw a bargain and had it on their stalls among the bags of sugar, selling at ten times the local price to the army of aid workers with access to hard currency. A reprint was paid for in dollars in Geneva, thanks to a creative accountant at the World Lutheran Federation office in Kampala.

Where was this world-wide organisation based? At our tenth anniversary there was a friendly article in *The Financial Times* (25 February 1995) in their series called 'Minding your own business'. It finished: 'Africa has suffered a books famine for a decade. The managing director of John Murray, publishers of Livingstone, and other publishers, told [James Currey] "Your books are everywhere".' There was a picture of 'The home office' with James and Clare Currey in the Islington basement flat with books shelved precipitously from floor to ceiling. The flat's back garden was a delight for lunches with authors who had just flown in from Baltimore or Botswana. I was a twelve- minute bicycle ride from the School of Oriental and African Studies in Bloomsbury. A Zambian postmaster in the Caledonian Road looked after our complicated worldwide parcels of manuscripts and books.

We had started at a moment when it was possible to have inexpensive access to the wonders of small office technology. Our communications hub ran through a manhole in the square outside which always seemed to have post office engineers garnering their multi-coloured wires as the phones were cut off for another day; yearly the telephones improved and became less expensive. Our student son haggled for a photocopier. Our student daughter pasted up illustrated books. Telexes, the crude text messages of their time, were phoned from an agency. Fax enabled us to have page proofs of a history of Ethiopia corrected in spite of the Red Terror in Addis. From the far side of America, at 3 a.m. a roll of fax sheets would pour down on to me asleep on a mattress on the floor. Above all it was the time when computers reached the small office. When we were joined by Keith Sambrook, my old Heinemann boss, cash flow spread sheets were late night labours in pencil with endless rubbing out. Clare Currey taught Keith Sambrook and me to write our own letters on Alan Sugar's Amstrads. When she broke her ankle we could magically transfer her early Dell computer to the country so she could continue working at our Hertfordshire water mill.

We interviewed Lynn Taylor, now our chief editor, in 1990; it was her daughter Nyamoi in her Moses basket who got her the job. On her first morning at work we were showing her how to listen to the answerphone messages and the first was a bomb threat. The police thought it was an Irish accent. We believed that it was Kenyans who objected to our co-publishing the exile Ngugi with Henry Chakava, another former Heinemann colleague in Nairobi.

At our tenth anniversary celebrations we published two new titles including one on African prophets edited by Douglas Johnson, who was then teaching at St Antony's College in Oxford. We did remember to bring the contract to the party for him to sign. On the way back to Oxford, Douglas's wife Wendy James, who was to become Professor of Social Anthropology, said that James Currey Publishers was providing such a service to Africanists that it must survive. We had only survived with Clare Currey's careful management of our marginal resources. The moment of greatest danger had been when only three years into our business, in the week of the great storm, J. M. Dent, whose warehouse distributed our books, went bust after the dollar and markets crashed on 'Black Monday' in 1987 owing us three months' turnover.

It is all very well to start a firm and take on authors, but what do you do next? Soon after the tenth anniversary, I was walking with David Philip, a leading publisher of the South Africa resistance, across the sand-dunes with the sun shining on the distant mountains of Cape Point, when he said 'What are you going to do with the firm?' He and his wife Marie Philip emphasised that you must have management accounts and a portrait of the business ready for prospective purchasers. During the mid-nineties we did put out feelers to both firms and individuals. We started serious discussions with Douglas Johnson and decided that we would set about working together to assess the possibilities of expanding the list. He came from a publishing family and his knowledge of Sudan and north-eastern Africa provided a web of new connections for the firm. He rapidly made an input into the next generation of books. Negotiations then began for him to take over the firm in stages.

It made sense for everybody to move the business to Oxford, where Douglas lived. Lynn Taylor had been twice to interviews for jobs in Oxford because that was where she wanted to live. Douglas Johnson lifted us out of our Islington basement 'publishing flat' into a fine four-square 'publishing house', along the road from the flooding Thames and a little way past Oxford Railway station. We could continue the tradition of office lunches with authors in the courtyard and kitchen. There was a flat upstairs for Clare Currey and myself to stay during the working week. Everybody could cycle to work.

There were other good reasons for being in Oxford. African Studies was building up to take off in the new century to become the second largest postgraduate course in the whole University. It was a period of energetic expansion and we quickly doubled the number of titles that we had been publishing. Terry Ranger, Rhodes Professor of Race Relations at Oxford, continued to publish on Zimbabwe and to bring in postgraduates writing on southern Africa. Douglas Johnson's contacts led to many new titles in the Eastern African studies. Work by outstanding younger scholars like Harvard's Emmanuel Kwaku Akyeampong expanded our range on West Africa. There were constant reprints of contentious titles in African Issues such as *Africa Works*, *Famine Crimes*, *The Criminalisation of the State in Africa* and Douglas Johnson's own *The Root Causes of Sudan's Civil Wars*. Basil Davidson and Ali

FORTY BOOKS FOR FORTY YEARS

Mazrui, two presenters of major TV series on Africa, treated us as their special publishers.

Lynn Taylor expanded the list of criticism of African literature which HEB Inc was selling in the US alongside Heinemann's African Writers Series. A detailed task was the key reference volume *The Companion to African Literatures*; I use it regularly and scarcely ever find an error in its packed pages. She also published biographies of *Chinua Achebe* and *Sembene*, the Senegalese novelist and film maker, and developed a pioneering list of highly illustrated books on African film.

In 1999 we completed the English language edition of the UNESCO *General History of Africa* with the publication of the thousand page paperback, Volume Eight, edited by Ali Mazrui. The *History* took thirty years of planning, writing and editing by scholars from Africa and the rest of world, working in Arabic, French, English and Portuguese. There are editions in many languages including Chinese, Japanese, Russian, French and Portuguese. In 1980 I had secured the lucrative contract for the English language hardback edition for Heinemann. In 1985, the first year of our new business, UNESCO asked us to publish eight paperback volumes of the *History* because they knew that I would arrange co-publishing deals with seven publishers in Africa. There was a happy symmetry to sums quoted to me by the Papal Nuncio from Malta, who said that when the project was planned in 1971 the Shah's widow had given $1,500, that the Vatican had given $15,000 and that Ghaddafy, who had removed King Idris two years before and had African ambitions, gave $1,500,000. In 2000 UNESCO organised a week-long conference of African historians and their publishers in Tripoli to mark the completion of the project. On the sixth day, without any hint, we were flown inland to Ghaddafy's marquee in the Sirte desert so that our authors Alan Ogot from Kenya and Adu Boahen from Ghana could present the history of the *History* to Ghaddafy, flanked by Amazon guards under the sumptuous but mended bedouin carpets which lined the tent. We felt rather like John Murray's author Speke crawling before the Kabaka in nineteenth-century Uganda. The assembled African presidents past and present and the Spanish head of UNESCO did not quite have to prostrate themselves as Ghaddafy growled his response against the rattle of a mounting sandstorm.

We are delighted that, within the Boydell & Brewer tent, the future of our twenty-five year old company has been secured.

UNIVERSITY OF ROCHESTER PRESS

The idea of a scholarly press for the University of Rochester arose (almost certainly not for the first time) in the 1988–89 academic year as part of the ongoing evaluation of academic programs. Although the Rochester faculty were prodigious producers of scholarly work with various university presses around the nation, it seemed as if the University of Rochester was missing one element that would contribute to scholarship nationally and internationally. The initial thoughts about establishing such a press emerged in conversations between President Dennis O'Brien and Provost Brian J. Thompson. And, as they tried out the idea on faculty leaders, it was clear that others wholeheartedly shared their enthusiasm. A press would enhance the University's contributions to the world of scholarship and, strategically, would add particular value if it were to publish in fields where the University was already strong.[40] It was also important that the press be related to the whole University and have a direct coupling to all of the colleges and schools – hence the concept that, if formed, the enterprise would be the responsibility of the provost's office. The press would publish in academic disciplines relating to the strengths of the University, with contributions from scholars around the world as well as from the University faculty.

An alternative to raising a sizeable endowment for the press–a course of action not available at the time – would be to use the University's regular internal accounts to provide the start-up funding and to bear the annual costs. These costs would start to be covered once books had been published and sold. At the time, however, many universities (including Rochester) were facing considerable budgetary constraints, and looking at comparable presses at other universities, it was unlikely that the operation would generate sufficient annual revenues to cover annual costs, let alone return the original investment.

With neither an endowment nor a sizeable operating budget from institutional coffers a ready possibility, the University began to explore different models, such as contractual arrangements with other scholarly publishers and, particularly, with other university presses. The challenge of such arrangements was

---

[40]   During such discussions O'Brien and Thompson were actually reminded by colleagues with long memories that there was once a University of Rochester Press. That operation had been based in the university's library and had "published" the Microcard Series, containing material previously published in print form as well as a series of theses that had not been formally published. It flourished from 1953 until the late 1970s, when the technology, akin to microfiche, became outdated.

that establishing a press would require significant financial investment from the University's partner; even with reduced annual costs, one or another of the parties involved would inevitably be exposed to financial risk.

But O'Brien, Thompson and others were determined not to give up on a good idea. Would some small, high-quality scholarly press be willing to become a strategic business partner? After a few inconclusive conversations with other entities, a group of faculty including professors Thomas Hahn and Russell Peck of the English department – significantly involved with medieval history and literature – suggested approaching Boydell & Brewer, Ltd, a British company privately owned and with a strong reputation for publishing serious scholarly work. Thus an introduction was made and a meeting scheduled in Rochester to discuss the possibilities with Derek Brewer and Richard Barber. The firm already had an American subsidiary, Boydell & Brewer, Inc, established in May 1986 to sell directly to the scholarly community in the United States. After further discussion, both sides enthusiastically agreed that they had found the perfect strategic partner for their respective objectives. The partnership needed careful definition. The editorial board of the University of Rochester Press (URP) would take full responsibility for determining the scope of the publishing profile in various disciplines, approving series editors and any series advisory boards. The URP editorial director would bring to the editorial board, for discussion and decision, proposals that the editor had accepted for consideration and that had undergone peer review. This is, of course, standard practice for any university press, but was spelled out in detail to underscore the way in which editorial decisions remained under University direction despite the arrangement with an outside publishing house for production, marketing, and distribution. The editorial board, made up largely of University faculty, was to be appointed by the provost and chaired by the provost or the provost's nominee. The University did, however, also wish to get professional input from their partner, and it was agreed that Boydell & Brewer Ltd should nominate 'two qualified persons to serve on the editorial board.' The editorial board is also responsible for the selection of the editorial director.

Once a manuscript had been approved, manuscript editing would be the responsibility of the Press editor, and then the Boydell & Brewer staff members would oversee production management, printing, warehousing, invoicing and accounting services, marketing, promotion and sales, and distribution to a worldwide market. Boydell & Brewer would bear all the costs incurred in fulfilling these obligations, and would retain the revenue from sales, returning to the University a negotiated percentage of its income from worldwide sales of URP books. The University would provide and pay for suitable offices and facilities on University grounds, and also support a limited amount of secretarial support service and a phone line.

The partnership formally came into being on September 1, 1989. Derek Brewer and Richard Barber were appointed to the editorial board as Boydell's representatives. The agreement called for the editorial board to recommend the appointment of the Press's editor. Until such time as the editor might be appointed and employed full time by the University, the appointee would be employed by Boydell & Brewer at their expense. However, the editor also would have a non-stipendiary appointment from the University to recognize that he or she was serving at the pleasure of the editorial board. Once the Press had achieved a sufficiently large turnover, the editorial directorship was to be transferred to the university payroll, and the percentage of sales paid to the University would be increased accordingly.

All in all, it was an unusual way for a university to start a scholarly press – without first raising a sustaining endowment or preparing to incur substantial operational costs. It relied on the good fortune of finding just the right partner, in this case an internationally established scholarly publisher looking for a foothold in the United States. Over the years, the arrangement has proven its considerable benefits both to the University and to Boydell & Brewer, and it still operates under the terms of the original agreement.

The Press was fortunate to get off to a good start with a series of volumes drawn from the distinguished content of the *Journal of the History of Ideas*, whose editor, Donald Kelley, was at the University, and the list was quickly strengthened by the purchase of fifty-two titles from University of Michigan Research Press, which was scaling back its book activities. This brought the first books on music, which was to become a mainstay of the Press's publishing activities. 'Eastman Studies in Music', under the editorship of Ralph Locke, is the jewel in the crown among the current series issued by the Press, with over sixty titles in print, and a long forward list. Combined with the strength of the Boydell Press's more general music books, and with the Toccata Press and Plumbago Press imprints which Boydell distribute, this represents a formidable force in the music publishing world.

There is a similar synergy between 'Rochester Studies in African History and the Diaspora', edited by Toyin Falola, and the James Currey list from the UK publishing operation. The two imprints operate at different levels, URP offering monographs and conference proceedings, largely in hardback, while James Currey offers predominantly shorter, more topical books, mostly in paperback. James Currey's excellent contacts in Africa mean that URP's books, despite their price, get the best possible exposure there.

In the early years, it was still feasible to publish hardback books covering the edited proceedings of major conferences in the sciences and medicine, particularly those where the University's senior faculty were involved in their direction. However, major scientific journals were already seen as the key medium of interchange of knowledge, and the traditional publication of conferences as peer-reviewed and edited books was replaced by camera-ready papers in paperback, published as a record of proceedings with minimal editorial intervention, and hence not suitable for the Press. URP did have an early success with John R. Huizenga's account of his investigation into the supposed 'nuclear reaction in a test-tube' that hit the headlines; *Cold Fusion* attracted considerable interest, bringing the Press to the attention of a wider audience.

At the end of URP's first decade, three further series, all in history, were started: Rochester Studies in Medical History, Changing Perspectives on Early Modern Europe, and Rochester Studies in Central Europe. The prestigious series of *Proceedings in Parliament*, covering the period of the English Civil War, was acquired from Yale. And two additional series have recently been launched, Gender and Race in American History and Eastman/Rochester Studies in Ethnomusicology.

But not all the Press's books are confined to series, though these are the major part of its production. A number of handsome art history volumes, many of them in collaboration with the University's Memorial Art Gallery, have added a further dimension, while the Press also provides a service for the publication of books about the University itself which need to pass through the editorial process and gain board approval, with production to a high standard, but which are intended for distribution rather than sale. This is done under the Meliora Press imprint.

Both the University of Rochester Press and the US sales activities of Boydell & Brewer Inc have expanded dramatically since 1989. The key figure in all this has been Brian Thompson, who has steered it through the often difficult waters of growth and development, first as Provost, then as chair of the editorial board and director of Boydell & Brewer Inc. He has seen many changes over twenty years; three editorial directors have come and gone, and the right organisational framework has taken time to evolve; but from these ups and downs has emerged the excellent team now in place, led by Suzanne Guiod as editorial director, with Robert Kraus, formerly associate Vice-President of the University, as chair of the editorial board.

Based on the official twentieth anniversary history of the University of Rochester Press by Brian J. Thompson

ACKNOWLEDGEMENTS

Boydell & Brewer has been remarkably fortunate in the loyalty and versatility of its employees, particularly their readiness to learn new skills. Pru Harrison, the firm's first employee, still does valuable freelance work for us, and her first colleague, Pam Cope, continues to copy-edit our more problematic titles. Joan Jordan has held the administration of the firm together for twenty-five years with remarkable cheerfulness and precision. Others, some equally long-serving, have started at the bottom of the ladder and have become managers, typesetters, and computer programmers. Vanda Andrews has been with us almost as long as Joan Jordan, and manages the copy-editors and typesetters; Elaine Townsend has become our highly skilled in-house compositor. Alison Coles will take over the firm's computer programming next year, using the experience of the last fifteen years. On the warehouse side, one family from the local village have largely staffed and managed it throughout its existence, and Lindsey Lain has been in charge for the past thirty years.

The editorial side was hugely strengthened with the arrival of Derek Brewer. I am conscious that I have perhaps not emphasised enough his role in the company in the preceding pages. He not only brought an extraordinary wealth of academic experience and a broad curiosity about the wider world of publishing, but was also endlessly patient with the trials and tribulations of the business affairs of the company, which must have seemed a distraction from its real purpose. He was ably supported in practical matters by Caroline Palmer, who again learned her skills on the job, beginning as an editorial trainee. We owe a great deal to our outside advisers and editors, but they need in-house support: Ellie Ferguson, who came to us as a personal assistant, rose to the challenge of taking over the Tamesis list.

Brian Thompson's role in the creation of University of Rochester Press has been chronicled above, but his interest in the firm as a whole has been a major influence in shaping its development in the last two decades. Like Derek, his contribution has been much greater than his immediate responsibilities.

As the firm has grown, so we have moved towards employing professionals with wider experience of the publishing world, and they have contributed to our success in recent years. A list of our current staff follows: it is they, under the leadership of Peter Clifford and Sue Smith, who will take the company forward into its fifth decade.

Finally, three personal notes. Going back to the beginnings of the company, Sam Wilson has been chairman from the outset; his lawyer's caution combined with an unshaken belief in the value of Boydell & Brewer has been of inestimable value in terms of support, while Bim Wilson has run an excellent warehouse very much tailored to the company's needs for all but three years of its existence. Perhaps it helps that we were all at school together at the age of seven …

When Helen was working as publicity manager at André Deutsch, John Updike inscribed a copy of *Couples* to her: 'To Helen, without whose skills this book would not have sold 200 copies.' Without her presence, Boydell & Brewer would not have flourished as it has.

Boydell & Brewer Directors, Staff and Editorial Advisers 2009

Group Board

Sam Wilson, *chairman*
Richard Barber, *group managing director*
Peter Clifford, *managing director, Boydell & Brewer Ltd*
Sue Smith, *managing director, Boydell & Brewer Inc*
Professor Brian Thompson, *non-executive director*
Ewen Stamp, *finance director*
Michael Brewer, *non-executive director*

Boydell & Brewer Ltd staff

Michael Richards, *sales & marketing director*
Mike Webb, *production director*
Caroline Palmer, *editorial director*
Joan Jordan, *administration and HR director*
Wendy Ellis, *finance and accounts director*

Michael Middeke, *senior commissioning editor*
Ellie Ferguson, *managing editor, Tamesis and Gallica*
Lynn Taylor, *managing editor, James Currey*

Rachel Reeder, *editions coordinator*

Vanda Andrews, *origination manager*
Elaine Townsend, *typesetting executive*

Sean Andersson, *sales & marketing manager*
Franziska Scheithauer, *sales & marketing assistant*
Amanda Davidson, *sales & marketing assistant*

Rohais Haughton, *assistant editor*
Catherine Larner, *assistant editor*

Moira Jordan, *customer services manager*
Amy Rowland, *customer services support assistant*
Jo Payne, *accounts assistant*

Boydell & Brewer Ltd external advisers

Peter Sowden, *freelance commissioning editor, modern history*
Bruce Phillips, *consultant editor, music*
Stephen Hart, *consultant editor, Tamesis*
Sarah Kay, *consultant editor, Gallica*
Douglas Johnson, *general editor, James Currey*

Boydell & Brewer Inc staff

Jim Walker, *editorial director, Camden House*
Susan Bain, *sales & marketing director*

Eloise Puls, *accounts & office manager*
Otto Bruno, *customer service representative*
Jennifer Shannon, *invoicing specialist*

Jane Best, *production editor, Camden House*
Tracey Engel, *production editor, URP*

Maureen Manley, *sales & marketing associate*
Jennifer Ostromecki, *sales & marketing coordinator*

Ryan Peterson, *associate managing editor*

Boydell & Brewer Ltd external advisers
Jim Hardin, *consultant editor, Camden House*

Group services

Alison Coles, *database manager*
Joan Simpson, *web manager*

University of Rochester

Suzanne Guiod, *editorial director, URP*